# Agentic Revenue Systems

How Autonomous Execution Redesigns the Modern Revenue Organization

By Tim Cortinovis

**Agentic Revenue Systems**



Publisher: Wordlab Publishing.

ISBN 979-8-90329-586-9

# Contents

# The Risk of Standing Still

There are moments in business when improvement is optional.

And there are moments when redesign is mandatory.

This is the latter.

For decades, revenue leadership has been a human coordination problem.

- Hire strong sellers.
- Install a CRM.
- Layer in dashboards.
- Coach harder.
- Inspect pipeline.

- Push at the end of the quarter.

The system was fragile, but it worked.

Or at least it worked well enough.

Today, that architecture is breaking.

Not because sales talent has declined.

Not because markets have become irrational.

But because execution speed, signal complexity, and buyer expectations have outpaced human orchestration.

The uncomfortable truth is this:

Revenue organizations built for manual coordination cannot compete with organizations built for autonomous execution.

And most leaders have not yet internalized what that means.

## The Quiet Shift Most Leaders Underestimate

AI is not the disruption.

Autonomy is.

Many executives still frame the moment as "adding AI tools."

They deploy email assistants, forecasting plugins, enrichment engines.

They improve pieces of the machine.

But their operating model remains unchanged.

Deals still depend on heroic sellers.

Forecasts still depend on manager intuition.

Cross-functional friction still delays execution.

Data remains fragmented.

The tools evolve.

The system does not.

That gap is where companies begin to fall behind.

Not loudly.

Quietly.

Quarter by quarter.

## The Second-Order Effect You Cannot Ignore

When a competitor builds an autonomous revenue system, three things happen:

1. Execution latency drops.
2. Signal detection improves.

3. Human capacity reallocates to high-leverage work.

The result is not incremental improvement.

It is structural advantage.

They spot deal risk earlier.

They surface expansion opportunities automatically.

They eliminate internal friction.

They convert insight into action without waiting for meetings.

Meanwhile, organizations still dependent on human inspection cycles operate in slower loops.

And in competitive markets, slower loops lose.

This is not a technology race.

It is a systems race.

The companies that redesign their revenue architecture will compound advantage.

The companies that merely automate tasks will compound complexity.

## The Illusion of Safety

The greatest strategic risk right now is not adopting the wrong AI tool.

It is believing that incremental optimization is enough.

Many leaders feel temporarily safe because their pipeline is stable.

Because their team is strong.

Because revenue has not yet declined.

But competitive advantage rarely collapses overnight.

It erodes.

Quietly.

The first signs are subtle:

- Forecast confidence weakens.
- Rep productivity plateaus.
- Tool sprawl increases.
- Data trust declines.
- AI pilots stall.

Individually, each symptom feels manageable.

Collectively, they signal architectural fragility.

The danger is not visible failure.

It is invisible stagnation.

## The Leadership Shift

This book is not about adopting AI.

It is about redefining your role as a revenue leader.

In the previous era, excellence meant being a strong operator and motivator.

In the next era, excellence will mean being a systems architect.

You will need to design:

- Clear autonomy boundaries.
- Human-in-the-loop control layers.
- Unified data foundations.
- Cross-functional orchestration.
- Governance that scales with intelligence.

This is not a technical responsibility.

It is a strategic one.

Boards will not ask whether you implemented AI.

They will ask whether you built a predictable, scalable revenue engine.

There is a difference.

## The Cost of Not Reading This Book

If you ignore this shift, three risks compound:

- You will overinvest in tools and underinvest in architecture.
- You will create AI noise without AI leverage.
- You will slowly cede structural advantage to competitors who redesign first.

Falling behind in this transition will not look dramatic.

It will look like:

- Slightly lower win rates.
- Slightly longer sales cycles.
- Slightly less forecast accuracy.
- Slightly higher cost of acquisition.

Until slightly becomes materially.

And by then, redesign is more expensive.

## Why This Book Matters

*Agentic Revenue Systems* does something rare.

It does not promise magic.

It does not sell hype.

It reframes revenue as a system-level design problem.

It exposes why most AI initiatives stall.

It provides mental models for levels of autonomy.

It offers a blueprint for moving from inspection-based management to orchestrated execution.

Most importantly, it gives you language.

Language to align your board.

Language to reassure your team.

Language to lead transformation rather than react to it.

## A Final Observation

In every major technological shift, the winners were not the companies with the earliest access to tools.

They were the companies that redesigned their operating systems first.

Autonomous revenue systems will define the next competitive frontier.

You can experiment around the edges.

Or you can architect the core.

This book is for leaders who understand the difference.

And who intend to lead it.

# Part I

# The Shift — From Human Coordination to Governed Autonomy

# Chapter 1

# From Heroic Selling to Agentic Systems

## The Hero Rep Was Never the Strategy. He Was the Patch.

Most revenue organizations do not run on process.

They run on exceptions.

A deal goes dark. A top rep resurrects it. Procurement stalls. Someone "knows a person." Forecast slips. The VP leans on three champions and drags the quarter across the line.

This has been mislabeled as excellence.

It is not excellence. It is containment.

The heroic selling model is what companies use when their revenue architecture cannot execute reliably on its own. The hero is the compensating mechanism for a system that does not close loops fast enough, detect weak signals early enough, or coordinate work precisely enough.

For a long time, this was survivable.

It is no longer competitive.

## What Actually Broke

The old model assumed three things that are now structurally false:

1. **Execution could be managed through inspection.** Weekly pipeline reviews, quarterly push rituals, and postmortems were acceptable control systems when the world moved slower than the meeting cadence.
2. **Signals were scarce.** Reps could "feel" the deal because the number of interactions, stakeholders, and channels was limited enough to hold in human working memory.
3. **Coordination was a human advantage.** The best organizations were simply the ones that communicated better across sales, marketing, and revenue operations.

Now the buyer journey is multi-threaded, the data exhaust is continuous, and the cost of waiting a week to respond to risk is measurable.

Revenue has become a latency game.

And the heroic model is a latency machine.

## The Real Divide: Activity Management vs. Execution Architecture

Most "modern" revenue stacks still preserve the same underlying operating model:

- Humans observe.
- Humans interpret.
- Humans decide.
- Humans execute.
- Managers inspect the residue.

Tools may accelerate pieces of that loop. But the loop remains human-timed.

An agentic revenue system changes the loop itself.

It does not merely make humans faster. It makes execution autonomous inside defined boundaries, with controls that management can audit and override.

This is the distinction leaders keep missing because they are still shopping for features instead of designing an operating system.

## Definition: What an Agentic Revenue System Is

An **agentic revenue system** is a goal-directed execution architecture that:

- Detects revenue signals continuously across channels and systems.
- Decides what action to take based on rules, context, and learned patterns.
- Acts by orchestrating work across sales, marketing, and RevOps workflows.
- Escalates exceptions to humans with context, options, and recommended next steps.
- Closes the loop by measuring outcomes and updating priorities without waiting for a meeting.

It is not a chatbot bolted onto CRM.

It is not automation that fires when a field changes.

It is not "AI for sales."

It is a system that executes revenue intent—autonomously—under governance.

## Why Autonomy Beats Heroism

The hero model concentrates capability inside individuals.

Agentic systems institutionalize capability inside the architecture.

That single shift produces three compounding advantages.

### 1) Latency Collapses

Heroic selling requires a person to notice, care, decide, and act.

Agentic execution compresses the time between signal and response.

Not because it "works harder." Because it operates continuously. No Monday morning required.

### 2) Attention Becomes Systemic

In the old system, attention is allocated by gut instinct, rep confidence, and political gravity.

In an agentic system, attention is allocated by risk, propensity, and priority—at scale.

This is not about being right more often. It is about being blind less often.

### 3) Human Judgment Moves Up the Stack

When the system handles orchestration, humans stop spending prime cognitive hours on coordination theater:

- "Did we follow up?"
- "Who owns the next step?"
- "Why is this stuck?"
- "Can someone update Salesforce?"

Humans return to what they are uniquely good at: negotiation, narrative, trust, and complex trade-offs.

The irony is that autonomy does not remove humans.

It removes wasteful human placement.

## What the Data Says When Companies Actually Do This

The shift becomes obvious when you look at where the reported gains come from. These are not "better email templates." The gains show up where systems execute, not where individuals hustle.

### ZoomInfo Copilot: Win Rates Improve When the System Prevents Deal Leaks

In deployments described around ZoomInfo Copilot, autonomous agents monitor pipeline conditions, flag degradation early, and ensure opportunities receive appropriate attention. Reported outcomes include **41% higher close rates** and **47% productivity gains**, with reps freeing **12 hours per week** for higher-value work [https://www.momentum.io/blog/future-autonomous-revenue-operations].

This is the pattern: win rates rise when the organization stops relying on individual vigilance as its primary control mechanism.

### SuperAGI GTM Agents: Revenue Lifts When Outbound Becomes an Execution Engine

Case studies cited for SuperAGI describe agentic workflows that run outbound, lead nurturing, and personalization as a coordinated system. Reported results include a **25% sales increase** and **30% shorter sales cycles**, with conversion improvements in the **20–40%** range across teams [https://web.superagi.com/case-studies-in-agentic-gtm-real-world-examples-of-how-autonomous-ai-agents-boost-sales-and-marketing-efficiency/].

Notice what changed. Not the brand voice. Not the rep scripts.

The operating model changed: outreach and follow-through moved from "best effort" to "continuous execution."

### Zams: Leakage Shrinks When Systems Coordinate the Quarter, Not Humans

Zams describes agentic automation that optimizes pipeline, scores deals, generates outreach, and coordinates actions across the revenue motion. Reported impact includes reducing revenue leakage by **4%** and unlocking **$775K** in value in specific cases [https://zams.com/blog/agentic-automation-in-action-enterprise-case-studies-that-prove-roi].

Leakage is what heroic selling normalizes.

A hero rescues the quarter and everyone celebrates. Meanwhile the system quietly bleeds in places no one has time to look.

Agentic systems look.

### Gong: Coaching Stops Being an Event and Becomes a Control Layer

Gong's revenue intelligence approach, as described in examples of agentic AI, emphasizes continuous interaction analysis—turning episodic coaching and consulting into ongoing system feedback [https://www.getmonetizely.com/articles/33-examples-of-agentic-ai-turning-professional-services-into-recurring-revenue].

This matters structurally: when performance improvement becomes continuous instrumentation rather than sporadic intervention, you reduce dependence on managerial heroics.

Managers stop playing detective.

They start designing the guardrails.

### SalesPlay Autonomous SDRs: Top-of-Funnel Scales Without Headcount as the Limiting Factor

SalesPlay is cited among autonomous SDR examples delivering **340% Year 1 ROI** and increasing lead volume by **2.3x** per rep (with reports ranging up to 3x) through automated prospecting and qualification [https://www.marketsandmarkets.com/AI-sales/top-5-autonomous-sdr-agents].

This is not a "productivity hack."

It is the decoupling of pipeline creation from hiring velocity.

And once that decoupling happens, your growth constraints shift permanently.

## Why Tools Don't Create This Shift

Most organizations will try to buy their way into autonomy with an "AI layer."

They will get more dashboards, more summaries, more suggested emails.

And the quarter will still be saved by the same three people.

Because the constraint is not insight. It is execution.

The modern revenue stack is saturated with information. But information does not move deals. Orchestration does.

Tools generate options.

Agentic systems generate outcomes—within defined constraints.

## The New Leadership Job: From Activity Governor to System Architect

In the heroic era, management meant:

- Driving compliance.
- Inspecting activity.
- Enforcing process.
- Motivating through pressure.

In the agentic era, leadership means:

- **Designing autonomy boundaries:** what the system can execute without permission.
- **Defining escalation logic:** what constitutes an exception worth human judgment.
- **Establishing control layers:** auditability, reversibility, and governance over actions.
- **Building cross-functional circuits:** marketing, sales, and RevOps as a single execution fabric.
- **Measuring system health:** latency, leakage, coverage, and compounding effects—not just activity counts.

This is not a technical job. It is an architectural one.

It requires the same posture shift that happened when finance moved from spreadsheets to integrated systems. The CFO did not become "more automated." Finance became governable at scale.

Revenue is next.

## The Hidden Failure Mode: Autonomy Without Governance

There is a predictable mistake leaders will make in this transition.

They will deploy autonomous execution without clear control surfaces.

Then they will call the resulting chaos "AI risk."

It is not AI risk. It is management abdication.

An agentic revenue system is not defined by how much it can do.

It is defined by how precisely it can be governed.

Autonomy without governance produces noise, brand drift, compliance exposure, and internal mistrust.

Governed autonomy produces structural advantage.

## The Inevitable Outcome

Over the next decade, the highest-performing revenue organizations will not be the ones with the most charismatic closers.

They will be the ones with the best execution engines.

The hero rep model will not disappear because leaders stop valuing talent.

It will disappear because talent will no longer be asked to compensate for architectural weakness.

Companies that redesign first will operate in faster loops, with lower leakage and higher coverage. Their human teams will do less coordination and more judgment. Their competitors will still be running on meetings.

And meetings do not scale.

Do you want to stay ahead of the wave?

The Agentic Revenue Brief

by Tim Cortinovis

How revenue leaders build autonomous execution engines — before their competitors do

Weekly clarity for **CROs, VPs Sales,** and **RevOps** leaders under pressure to deliver growth without adding headcount.

**Get the free Friday Brief**

**https://www.timcortinovis.com/tarb**

High-signal insights on autonomous revenue systems. No hype. No vendor fluff.

Your pipeline looks busy. Your forecast feels fragile. Your reps are drowning in tools.

AI is everywhere. Clarity is not.

Chapter 2

# The Hidden Cost of Tool Sprawl

## The Stack Didn't Get Smarter. It Got Louder.

Most revenue organizations did not "implement AI." They accumulated it.

They added it the way they added dashboards in the last era: as a surface layer on top of the same brittle operating system—broken processes, mismatched definitions, and data that no one fully trusts.

The result is predictable. Not transformation. A thicker stack. More surfaces. More alerts. More summaries. More "insight." Less control.

Tool sprawl is not an IT cleanliness issue. It is a revenue architecture failure. And it creates a specific set of structural costs that compound quietly—until the quarter starts slipping and no one can explain why.

## The Misdiagnosis: "We Have an AI Gap"

Most teams experiencing sprawl believe they have an adoption problem. They do not. They have an operating model problem.

When leaders say, "We need to get more out of AI," what they usually mean is:

- Our systems disagree with each other.
- Our teams are working around process instead of inside it.
- Our intelligence layer is built on unstable inputs.
- We cannot tell what is true without a meeting.

AI did not create those conditions. AI just makes them visible—then accelerates their consequences.

## The Structural Shift: From Systems of Record to Systems of Action

In the last era, revenue stacks were optimized for documentation. CRM as the ledger. BI as the scoreboard. Enablement as the library. If the data was imperfect, it was survivable. Humans compensated.

Agentic systems change the requirement. They do not just record work. They execute work.

Execution requires something your stack likely does not have: a coherent, governable truth that can safely produce action.

When you bolt "systems of action" on top of "systems of disputed record," the failure modes stop being annoying. They become operational. Your stack starts acting on contradictions.

## Why Tool Sprawl Explodes in Revenue Organizations

Revenue is uniquely vulnerable because it is cross-functional by nature and politically fragmented by design. Sales, marketing, CS, RevOps, finance—each team has its own tools, incentives, definitions, and tolerance for risk.

So sprawl doesn't look like one bad purchase. It looks like local optimization.

- Marketing buys an AI personalization platform.
- Sales adds an AI copilot.
- RevOps plugs in enrichment.
- CS stands up an agent for renewals.
- Finance builds its own forecasting logic.

Each decision is defensible. Collectively, they produce a system that cannot agree on what is happening, why it is happening, or what to do next.

This is not "innovation." It is parallel automation. And parallel automation is how organizations manufacture internal conflict at machine speed.

## The Three Failure Modes: Noise, Inconsistency, False Confidence

### 1) Noise: When the System Produces More Signals Than You Can Govern

Noise is not "too much data." Noise is *un-actionable output*. It's what happens when tools generate alerts, scores, summaries, and tasks faster than your organization can validate, route, and resolve them.

In sprawl conditions, noise doesn't stay in the UI. It becomes workflow. Your teams start doing work to manage the output of tools that were bought to reduce work.

The Zapier survey data captures the pattern: enterprises remain stuck at basic integration while unapproved usage proliferates—28% reported 10+ unapproved apps, and 31% discovered rogue AI tools monthly [https://zapier.com/blog/ai-sprawl-survey/]. That is not "experimentation." That is uncontrolled signal generation with no operating discipline.

Noise has a revenue signature:

- More time spent reconciling reports than acting on them.
- More time debating pipeline than moving it.
- More internal follow-up than customer follow-up.

When noise rises, leadership responds by adding "visibility." Which adds more tools. Which generates more noise. This is how stacks become self-thickening.

### 2) Inconsistency: When the Stack Can't Maintain a Single Reality

Inconsistency is the most expensive failure mode because it destroys coordination. It turns every cross-functional handoff into a negotiation.

Inconsistency shows up as:

- Different lead statuses depending on the system.
- Different attribution depending on the dashboard.
- Different forecast numbers depending on who exported last.
- Different "next best actions" depending on the copilot.

This is not a data hygiene issue. It is a semantic architecture issue. Your organization lacks enforced definitions and governed workflows, so every tool recreates reality in its own image.

Failure analyses consistently point to the same root: weak foundations—data, infrastructure, and process—prevent AI systems from reaching stable production value. Schellman cites that the majority of AI projects do not make it into production, driven by inadequate data and infrastructure readiness [https://www.schellman.com/blog/ai-services/ai-implementation-failures-in-real-world-deployments]. Service Innovation similarly highlights failure rates post-deployment and points to bad data as the dominant cause (with data issues representing the bulk of problems) [https://www.serviceinnovation.org/why-ai-projects-fail-or-succeed/].

In revenue teams, inconsistency has an executive-level symptom: you cannot speak cleanly to the board without first convening a war room. Not because you lack analytics. Because you lack alignment.

### 3) False Confidence: When Better Outputs Create Worse Decisions

False confidence is what kills companies that "look fine" right up until they miss. It's the most dangerous outcome of sprawl because it feels like progress.

A stack with ten AI layers can generate polished narratives:

- "Pipeline coverage is healthy."
- "This deal is 78% likely to close."
- "These accounts are warm."
- "Forecast variance is within tolerance."

But if those outputs are produced from inconsistent definitions, partial integrations, and ungoverned agent behavior, the polish becomes a liability. It anesthetizes leadership. It replaces investigation with belief.

Beam.ai describes the growth of "shadow AI" and unmonitored agents creating unpredictable data flows and material security exposure, including breach risk figures tied to blind spots in governance [https://beam.ai/agentic-insights/ai-agent-sprawl-new-shadow-it]. Revenue leaders should read that as an operating warning, not a security footnote:

unmonitored agents do not just leak data. They leak decisions.

False confidence produces a distinct behavior shift: leaders stop asking, "What would we need to verify this?" and start asking, "How do we scale it?" That is how sprawl becomes institutional.

## The Amazon Story Is Not About Bias. It's About Architecture.

Most executives remember the Amazon hiring AI episode as a cautionary tale about bias. The deeper lesson is more operational.

The model learned from historical patterns embedded in the system. The system produced outputs that were treated as guidance. Over time, the organization discovered the guidance was structurally wrong for its goals—and the program was abandoned [https://www.schellman.com/blog/ai-services/ai-implementation-failures-in-real-world-deployments].

Revenue organizations are currently building their own version of this failure:

- They train scoring and forecasting on historical deals shaped by inconsistent process.

- They use outputs to reinforce the same brittle behaviors.
- They call the result "AI insight."

Then they wonder why performance doesn't change.

When your history was produced by heroism, politics, and end-of-quarter theatrics, your models will faithfully learn heroism, politics, and end-of-quarter theatrics. Not because AI is flawed. Because your operating system is.

## The Unseen Cost: Tool Sprawl Creates Revenue Bottlenecks

Sprawl is not just extra spend. It creates bottlenecks in the revenue stack that aren't visible on a budget line.

Three bottlenecks show up repeatedly:

### Bottleneck A: Integration Drag

As tools proliferate, integration becomes the work. Not selling. Not messaging. Not customer outcomes. Integration.

Zapier's survey points to manual data movement persisting inside enterprises—teams still moving data by hand between systems, despite AI proliferation [https://zapier.com/blog/ai-sprawl-survey/]. That is the signature of a stack that has expanded faster than it has been integrated.

Integration drag produces a hard operational truth: your latency increases even while your tools promise speed.

### Bottleneck B: Governance Load

Every new AI layer adds an implicit governance requirement:

- What data can it access?
- What actions can it take?
- Who audits the outputs?
- What is the rollback path?
- What is the escalation logic?

Most organizations answer those questions informally. Until something breaks. Then they answer them under pressure.

Beam.ai's framing of agent sprawl emphasizes the need for centralized governance to map connections and audit outputs across departments [https://beam.ai/agentic-insights/ai-agent-sprawl-new-shadow-it]. That is not a "best practice." It is the price of operating agentic capacity without losing control.

### Bottleneck C: Decision Arbitration

When tools disagree, humans become arbitrators. Meetings become middleware.

This is why sprawl does not merely reduce efficiency. It increases management burden. Because the organization regresses to the oldest control layer available: executive attention.

## How Sprawl Fractures the Revenue Narrative

Boards do not fund tools. They fund predictability.

Tool sprawl attacks predictability by fragmenting the revenue narrative:

- Marketing says demand is strong.
- Sales says the top of funnel is noisy.
- CS says expansion is healthy.
- Finance says cash timing is slipping.
- RevOps says the data is "mostly accurate."

All of them can be correct inside their local tool environment. Collectively, they produce paralysis.

Nutanix describes this pattern directly: sales and marketing adopt duplicate AI tools without cohesion, resulting in fragmented insights and a harder-to-manage environment [https://www.nutanix.com/theforecastbynutanix/business/managing-enterprise-ai-sprawl]. This is what sprawl looks like in the day-to-day: multiple versions of "truth," each backed by a vendor dashboard.

Your competitors do not need better sellers to beat you in this environment. They need a cleaner system.

## A Diagnostic Lens: Quantifying Chaos in Your Current Revenue Stack

Most leaders ask the wrong diagnostic question: "How many tools do we have?"

Tool count is a weak indicator. A small number of poorly governed tools can create more chaos than a large number of tightly governed tools.

You need diagnostics that reveal structural brittleness. Use this lens.

### 1) Truth Count: How Many "Official" Numbers Exist?

Count the number of answers your organization can produce to each question:

- What is pipeline?
- What is qualified pipeline?
- What is forecast?
- What is CAC?
- What is churn risk?

If the answer depends on which system you open, your truth count is greater than one. Truth count > 1 predicts political forecasting and coordination drag.

### 2) Orchestration Coverage: What Percentage of Workflows Are End-to-End?

Map your critical revenue workflows: lead-to-meeting, meeting-to-opportunity, opportunity-to-close, close-to-onboard, onboard-to-expand.

For each, identify whether the workflow is:

- **End-to-end orchestrated** (single governed path)
- **Partially orchestrated** (handoffs via exports, Slack, email, or meetings)
- **Manually stitched** (humans as integration)

The Zapier survey's evidence of ongoing manual data transfer is a direct warning sign of low orchestration coverage [https://zapier.com/blog/ai-sprawl-survey/]. If humans are still moving data, your system is not integrated. It is narrated.

### 3) Action Permissioning: Who Can Trigger Revenue Actions?

List every system or agent that can:

- Send customer-facing communication
- Change opportunity stage
- Adjust routing
- Modify pricing or terms
- Commit forecast assumptions

If you cannot answer quickly, you do not have autonomy. You have uncontrolled automation. Beam.ai's warning about unmonitored agents is essentially a permissioning problem expressed at scale [https://beam.ai/agentic-insights/ai-agent-sprawl-new-shadow-it].

### 4) Exception Rate: How Often Do You Need a Meeting to Resolve the System?

Track how often execution stalls and requires human arbitration:

- Lead disputes
- Territory conflicts
- Attribution arguments
- Forecast overrides
- "We don't trust that score" emails

Exception rate is the operational cost of inconsistency. The higher it is, the more your organization is paying people to compensate for architectural gaps.

### 5) Production Ratio: How Many AI Initiatives Survive Contact With Reality?

Track AI pilots vs. systems that run the business.

Failure analyses highlight a familiar pattern: most AI initiatives never reach durable production, often due to data and infrastructure readiness gaps [https://www.schellman.com/blog/ai-services/ai-implementation-failures-in-real-world-deployments] [https://www.serviceinnovation.org/why-ai-projects-fail-or-succeed/]. If your organization runs many pilots and few productions, you don't have an innovation problem. You have a foundation problem.

## The Cure Is Not Consolidation. It's Governed Orchestration.

Most companies respond to sprawl with procurement theater:

- "Let's rationalize vendors."
- "Let's consolidate tools."
- "Let's negotiate better contracts."

That is cost control, not system design. You can consolidate and still keep the same architectural flaw: disconnected execution with ambiguous control.

The structural solution is governed orchestration:

- **A single execution fabric** that routes work across functions.
- **Declared definitions** enforced at the system level, not negotiated in meetings.
- **Explicit autonomy boundaries** defining what the system can do without permission.

- **Auditable control surfaces** with rollback paths and accountability.
- **Central visibility into workflows** so unapproved tools cannot silently become production dependencies.

Zapier's recommendation of central orchestration platforms for workflow visibility aligns with the operational need: governance requires observable workflow control, not scattered point solutions [https://zapier.com/blog/ai-sprawl-survey/]. Beam.ai's emphasis on centralized governance echoes the same requirement from a risk lens [https://beam.ai/agentic-insights/ai-agent-sprawl-new-shadow-it]. Nutanix's sprawl story reinforces that duplication across departments is not a tooling issue—it's the absence of an enterprise execution architecture [https://www.nutanix.com/theforecastbynutanix/business/managing-enterprise-ai-sprawl].

## The Forward Implication: Your Revenue Stack Is Becoming a Liability

In the manual era, a messy stack was tolerable. People compensated. They reconciled. They patched. They stayed late.

In the agentic era, a messy stack is operational risk. Because systems that act on your behalf will execute your contradictions at scale.

Tool sprawl is not a phase. It is a fork.

One path is continued accumulation: more tools, more noise, more inconsistency, more confidence built on thin reality. That path ends in slower loops and higher leakage—while competitors run tighter systems.

The other path is redesign: fewer truths, governed actions, and orchestration that collapses latency without sacrificing control.

The winning revenue organizations will not have the most AI. They will have the most governable execution.

Chapter 3

# Competing on Autonomous Execution

## The Old Competitive Story: "We Need Better Reps."

In most boardrooms, revenue performance still gets explained like a hiring problem.

"We need stronger closers."

"We need more outbound."

"We need a player-coach leader."

"We need to raise activity."

That story survived because it was directionally true in a world where execution capacity lived inside people. Sales was labor. Growth was labor scaled.

That era is over.

Not because talent stopped mattering. Because talent stopped being the bottleneck.

In modern B2B markets, the binding constraint is not persuasion. It is execution throughput under complexity. The company that can detect signals earlier, respond faster, and adapt its motion without human re-coordination will beat the company with the larger team and the louder activity.

## The New Competitive Unit: The Autonomous Revenue System

Companies are no longer competing on sales talent alone. They are competing on the quality of their autonomous execution architecture.

This is the shift most leaders misread. They think autonomy is about automating tasks. It is not. Autonomy is about changing what "capacity" means.

In the old model, capacity was headcount multiplied by effort. In the new model, capacity is system velocity multiplied by governance.

That is why the winners will not look like the companies with the most sellers. They will look like the companies with the shortest distance between signal and action—across the full revenue chain.

## System Velocity: The Metric That Replaces Brute Force

The language already exists, even if most teams use it like a dashboard KPI. SalesGlobe defines revenue velocity with a blunt formula:

**Revenue Velocity = (Opportunities × Deal Size × Win Rate) ÷ Cycle Length**
[https://www.salesglobe.com/blog/a-framework-for-performance-productivity-and-growth/]

Most organizations treat that equation as a report. High-performing organizations treat it as an operating design constraint.

Because every variable in that formula is now system-shaped:

- **Opportunities** are no longer "generated." They are routed, scored, and sequenced.
- **Deal size** is no longer "negotiated." It is packaged, priced, and expanded through controlled plays.
- **Win rate** is no longer "coached." It is reinforced through continuous signal capture and intervention.

- **Cycle length** is no longer "pushed." It is compressed by removing internal latency and buyer friction.

Brute force only influences velocity by adding more human output. Autonomous execution influences velocity by changing the shape of the system.

That is why autonomy compounds. Headcount does not.

## The Competitive Dynamic: Two Companies, Same Market, Different Physics

Put two competitors in the same category, selling to the same buyers, facing the same procurement friction.

Company A scales the old way: more reps, more sequences, more enablement sessions, more pipeline calls. They improve by adding labor. Their failure mode is familiar: rising cost, plateauing output, and management attention as the ultimate bottleneck.

Company B scales through autonomous execution: a governed system that detects intent signals, prioritizes accounts, orchestrates next actions, and escalates exceptions with context. They improve by upgrading the loop. Their failure mode is different: weak architecture creates chaos. But when they get it right, they move with a different set of constraints.

Over time, Company B does not merely "sell better." They operate faster. They learn faster. They waste less. They protect margin while increasing throughput.

This is what executives miss: the competition is no longer sales-versus-sales. It is loop-versus-loop.

## The Second-Order Effects Leaders Underestimate

Most teams look for first-order gains: time saved, emails written, meetings summarized. Those are rounding errors. The real advantage comes from second-order effects that reprice the business.

### Second-Order Effect #1: Speed Becomes a Margin Strategy

Speed is not a motivational virtue. It is an economic weapon.

A faster execution loop reduces cycle length, which directly increases revenue velocity and reduces cost of carry in pipeline. But more importantly, it reduces the tax you pay for internal coordination.

RapidCanvas frames the modern opportunity directly: reclaiming rep time, accelerating deal velocity, and reducing fragmentation—while driving outsized ROI because the system removes cross-tool drag rather than merely improving rep activity [https://www.rapidcanvas.ai/guides/a-blueprint-for-transformed-sales-performance-and-intelligence].

That matters because in most B2B organizations, the hidden cost is not tools. It is people acting as glue between tools: copying notes, reconciling fields, re-explaining context, re-creating intent.

Autonomous execution removes that glue-work. That is why speed shows up as margin.

### Second-Order Effect #2: Adaptability Becomes the New Moat

The old moat was positioning plus distribution. The new moat is adaptation velocity.

When markets shift—messaging fatigue, channel saturation, competitor moves—the question is not "do we know what changed?" Most teams can see the change. The question is "how fast can we reconfigure execution and propagate the new behavior?"

HivePerform highlights the operational reality: reply rates flatten, burnout rises, and brute force becomes obsolete because volume-based execution cannot adapt fast enough without breaking the team [https://www.hiveperform.com/resource-hub/what-top-cros-are-still-getting-wrong-about-sales-execution-in-2025].

Autonomous systems blunt this problem by systematizing learning:

- Signals update priorities continuously.
- Plays update in the workflow, not in a slide deck.
- Execution changes propagate without retraining the entire org by hand.

This is the unglamorous truth: adaptability is mostly a deployment problem. Autonomy turns adaptation into a system property.

### Second-Order Effect #3: Headcount Stops Being the Primary Growth Lever

In the old model, growth was gated by hiring velocity and ramp time. That gating created a predictable executive reflex: "add capacity."

Autonomous revenue operations change the gating mechanism. Momentum.io's roadmap for autonomous revenue ops describes phased adoption—prospecting, deal velocity, and operational automation—designed to reduce dependency on human throughput while increasing consistency through governance and iteration [https://www.momentum.io/blog/future-autonomous-revenue-operations].

This is not a productivity story. It is a constraint story.

When pipeline creation, follow-through, and risk detection become system behaviors, headcount becomes a strategic choice instead of an existential requirement. Your organization stops being sized by labor limits. It becomes sized by governance limits: how much autonomy you can safely run without losing control.

## The Case for "Less Volume, More Precision" Is Not Philosophical. It's Structural.

B2B outreach has been inflated by the same misconception: if results stall, push more activity.

Nectar Group's story is the more useful counterexample because it ties autonomy to outcomes that matter: improved lead quality (83%), higher reply rates (57%), and 5+ hours per rep freed—plus shorter cycles—by shifting from brute-force volume to data-driven, automated precision [https://www.nectargroup.co/blog/smarter-sales-growth-strategies-for-modern-teams].

Notice what that implies. If lead quality rises and the rep gains time back, you do not just get "more output." You get option value:

- You can redeploy time into late-stage strategy, not top-of-funnel labor.
- You can shrink the team without shrinking coverage.
- You can expand coverage without expanding burn.

That is why autonomous execution is a structural play. It creates choices your competitors do not have.

## Why "Headcount Brute Force" Fails Under Modern Complexity

Brute force fails for three reasons, and none of them are moral. They are mechanical.

### 1) Humans Cannot Run Continuous Control Loops

A weekly pipeline review is not a control system. It is delayed observation.

By the time the system notices risk, the buyer has already moved. The competitor has already engaged. Procurement has already set the frame.

Autonomous execution closes the loop at machine cadence while preserving human override. That is the point: continuous detection, bounded action, exception escalation.

### 2) More People Increases Coordination Load Faster Than Capacity

Every additional rep increases: handoffs, attribution disputes, process variance, forecasting variance, and managerial arbitration.

So the organization grows. But the system slows.

This is why companies feel "busier" right before they feel stuck. The system is producing motion without throughput.

### 3) Brute Force Inflates Cost Before It Inflates Revenue

Hiring is upfront cost. Pipeline is delayed payoff. In a noisy environment, much of that pipeline is synthetic. It looks like activity but does not convert.

Velocity-driven systems behave differently: they compress cycle length, raise win rate through earlier intervention, and reduce waste. They improve unit economics while they scale.

## The Operating Model Shift: From Reps as Producers to Reps as Governors of Exceptions

This shift makes people uncomfortable because it changes what "a great rep" does.

In autonomous execution, the system produces the baseline: routing, follow-ups, sequencing, reminders, risk flags, escalation packets, handoff triggers.

Humans stop being the primary engine of coordination. They become:

- **Deal strategists** at inflection points, not task runners across the entire cycle.
- **Trust carriers** in moments where credibility matters.
- **Negotiators** where trade-offs are non-linear.
- **Governors** of exceptions the system should not decide.

The rep is not replaced. The rep is repositioned.

And that repositioning is exactly how you win margin while growing. You stop paying premium human cognition to do clerical orchestration.

## The New Battleground: Execution Integrity

As more companies deploy autonomous capacity, the differentiation will not be "who has agents." It will be who can run autonomy without degrading trust.

Execution integrity has three components:

- **Truth integrity**: the system is anchored to governed definitions, not local dashboards.
- **Action integrity**: the system can act, but actions are permissioned, auditable, and reversible.
- **Learning integrity**: improvements propagate through workflows, not folklore.

This is where many teams will lose the plot. They will chase "more automation" and call the resulting friction "change management."

It is not change management. It is architectural debt showing up as operational drag.

## What Winning Looks Like in the Next Revenue Era

The next dominant revenue organizations will look calm, not frantic. Their dashboards will be quieter. Their meetings will be fewer. Their pipeline reviews will be shorter because the system already did the inspection.

They will measure what actually drives competitive advantage:

- **Signal-to-action latency**: how quickly intent becomes execution.
- **Loop closure rate**: how reliably next steps happen without human chasing.
- **Exception quality**: what gets escalated, how well it's packaged, how fast it resolves.
- **Velocity integrity**: whether speed comes from clarity or from chaos.

They will still hire great people. But they will not ask great people to compensate for a slow system. That is what mediocre companies do—then call it culture.

## The Inevitable Implication

In B2B, competition is consolidating around one structural advantage: autonomous execution with governance.

As that advantage spreads, the center of gravity moves: from activity to velocity, from volume to precision, from headcount to architecture.

The companies that treat autonomous execution as their operating system will compound speed, adaptability, and margin. The companies that treat it as a layer of tools will compound noise and management burden.

The market will not reward effort. It will reward throughput. And throughput now belongs to the system.

Chapter 4

# The 4 Levels of Sales Autonomy

## The Most Expensive Confusion in Revenue Leadership

Most leadership teams think they are debating "AI adoption." They are not. They are debating how much execution authority they are willing to move from humans into the system.

Until you name that transfer of authority, you cannot govern it. And if you cannot govern it, you cannot scale it.

This is why so many revenue organizations oscillate between two equally flawed states:

- **Manual heroics** dressed up as "high performance."
- **Chaotic automation** dressed up as "innovation."

Sales autonomy is the missing taxonomy. It turns autonomy from a vague ambition into a design ladder. Not "more AI." More controllable execution.

## The Autonomy Ladder: Four Levels, One Structural Direction

Autonomy progresses through four levels:

1. **Assisted Tasks**
2. **Guided Workflows**
3. **Semi-Autonomous Orchestration**
4. **Autonomous Execution with Human Supervision**

Each level increases the system's authority to move work forward without waiting for a human. Each level also increases the need for explicit governance: permissions, auditability, escalation logic, and rollback.

The point is not to "reach Level 4." The point is to match autonomy to risk, complexity, and your capacity to govern—then climb with discipline. The ladder is a map. It prevents two common executive failures:

- Buying tools that cannot change your operating model.
- Granting autonomy you cannot control.

## Level 1: Assisted Tasks

### What it is

Assisted Tasks is the earliest form of autonomy: the system helps humans act faster, but it does not run the work. Humans remain the workflow.

This is where most organizations start because it is politically easy. No process redesign. No permission design. No cross-functional alignment required. Just "help the rep."

### Typical indicators

- AI support that creates drafts, reminders, call summaries, or suggested next steps—without taking action.
- Rep-controlled goals with visibility layers: dashboards, targets, missions, personal scoreboards.
- Managers inspect outcomes, not execution in-flight.

SalesScreen's best-practice framing is representative of Level 1: reps set weekly "missions" (e.g., book 10 meetings), with manager visibility through dashboards—autonomy paired with accountability mechanisms rather than rigid command-and-control [https://www.salesscreen.com/blog/sales-autonomy/].

### What you gain (ROI pattern)

- **Local productivity**: less time wasted on clerical work.
- **Motivation uplift** when autonomy is framed as ownership with transparent measurement.
- **Faster onboarding** for the obvious tasks—because reps get prompts instead of guessing.

The returns here are real, but capped. Assistance improves output. It does not improve system reliability.

### Hidden failure mode

Level 1 creates an illusion of modernization. Executives see activity rise and assume execution improved. But the system still depends on two fragile things:

- Rep memory
- Manager inspection cycles

In other words: latency remains. Level 1 is helpful. It is not structural.

## Level 2: Guided Workflows

### What it is

Guided Workflows is where autonomy becomes an operating model decision. The system stops merely assisting tasks and starts shaping the path: capture, route, sequence, and enforce steps. Humans still do the selling. But they no longer invent the workflow every time.

### Typical indicators

- Automated lead capture and routing with defined handoffs.
- CRM syncing that reduces manual updates and enforces required fields at the moment of action.
- Playbooks embedded into the workflow: "when X happens, do Y."
- Manager visibility shifts from activity policing to flow monitoring.

Activepieces describes the practical center of gravity of Level 2: automated lead capture, task assignment, and CRM synchronization—removing manual glue-work and guiding execution through defined steps rather than rep improvisation [https://www.activepieces.com/blog/sales-automation-examples].

Highspot's workflow automation examples sit squarely in Level 2 as well: AI-driven follow-ups, recommended next steps, and post-call coaching tasks that reduce manual administration and routinize good execution [https://www.highspot.com/blog/sales-workflow-automation/].

### What you gain (ROI pattern)

- **Consistency**: fewer dropped handoffs, fewer forgotten follow-ups.
- **Ramp compression**: new reps inherit a working path instead of tribal knowledge.
- **Reduced manual error** in multi-step motions—especially at the boundaries between systems.

Level 2 ROI shows up as fewer leaks and fewer "we didn't know" moments. Not because people got better. Because the workflow got tighter.

### Risks leaders underestimate

- **Backlog risk**: automating intake without monitoring throughput creates pileups. The system "routes" work into a queue no one has capacity to clear. Activepieces flags the need to monitor automated pipelines to prevent workload backups [https://www.activepieces.com/blog/sales-automation-examples].

- **Compliance theater:** teams learn to complete fields to satisfy the workflow, not to reflect reality. Your CRM becomes cosmetically clean and strategically useless.

### The level-up decision

Level 2 forces a question most revenue teams avoid: Do we want a workflow that reflects reality, or reality that conforms to the workflow?

At this level, the workflow is no longer documentation. It is behavior control. And behavior control without truth produces a beautifully governed lie.

## Level 3: Semi-Autonomous Orchestration

### What it is

Semi-Autonomous Orchestration is where autonomy becomes competitive. The system begins coordinating work across steps and roles, not just within a single rep's task list. It prioritizes. It sequences. It triggers follow-through. It packages context. It escalates exceptions.

Humans still own outcomes. But the system owns flow.

### Typical indicators

- Automated follow-ups that happen because the system detected non-response, stage risk, or stakeholder gaps.
- Next-step recommendations derived from patterns, not just static rules.
- Coaching and enablement triggered by observed behavior (post-call, post-demo, post-procurement event).
- Work routed across functions: SDR → AE → SE → legal → finance, with less re-explaining.

Highspot explicitly bridges Levels 2 and 3: workflow automation that moves beyond basic enablement into AI-driven orchestration—follow-ups, task generation after calls, and prioritized actions that shift time away from administration and toward closing [https://www.highspot.com/blog/sales-workflow-automation/].

### What you gain (ROI pattern)

- **More time closing** because the system reduces coordination overhead.
- **Earlier risk detection** because orchestration watches more signals than any manager can.
- **Higher execution coverage**: more accounts get "good enough" follow-through, not just the ones with the loudest reps.

This is where ROI stops looking like "minutes saved" and starts looking like "deals that didn't die quietly."

### Risks leaders trigger themselves

- **Over-reliance**: teams stop developing judgment because the system always suggests the next move. Highspot warns about over-reliance without human oversight—an operational risk, not a philosophical one [https://www.highspot.com/blog/sales-workflow-automation/].
- **Orchestration without discipline**: autonomy amplifies both excellence and chaos. If fundamentals are weak—poor discovery, sloppy qualification—semi-autonomy just accelerates your mistakes.

TheSalesBlog frames the tension with unusual clarity: autonomy only works when paired with discipline; high performers can "color outside the lines," but ignoring fundamentals causes failure [https://www.thesalesblog.com/blog/sales-effectiveness-autonomy-vs-discipline].

### The level-up decision

Level 3 forces an executive trade:

- If you want orchestration, you must standardize definitions and escalation thresholds.
- If you want local freedom, you must accept system variance and higher exception load.

Most companies try to keep both. They end up with neither: local improvisation wrapped in automated noise.

## Level 4: Autonomous Execution with Human Supervision

### What it is

Level 4 is not "sales runs itself." It is a more mature claim: the system can execute revenue plays end-to-end inside defined boundaries, while humans supervise exceptions, policies, and trade-offs.

This is the difference between a system that recommends and a system that commits. Level 4 commits actions: outreach, task creation, routing decisions, meeting progression, handoff triggers, and operational updates—under permissioning. Humans intervene when the system hits a boundary or detects high-risk conditions.

The ONSA ladder frames this progression directly: an autonomy model that mirrors "self-driving" maturity, moving from manual work toward agentic execution [https://www.onsa.ai/sales-autonomy-ladder].

### Typical indicators

- **Defined action permissions**: the system can execute specific classes of actions without approval.
- **Auditable trails**: every action is attributable, reviewable, and reversible.
- **Supervision dashboards** oriented around exceptions, not activities.
- **Human role redesign**: reps and managers shift from doing the work to governing the work.

TheSalesBlog's framing becomes operationally relevant here: top performers pair autonomy with discipline, and the organization must ensure fundamentals remain intact even as execution becomes more independent [https://www.thesalesblog.com/blog/sales-effectiveness-autonomy-vs-discipline].

### What you gain (ROI pattern)

- **Execution continuity**: follow-through becomes systemic, not personality-dependent.
- **Lower leakage**: fewer deals die from neglect, delay, or internal handoff failure.
- **Scalable precision**: the organization can run more plays across more accounts without linear headcount growth.

Level 4 ROI is structural: predictability rises because the system controls the baseline. Humans stop being the glue. They become the governors.

### The only risk that matters: autonomy without governance

At Level 4, the primary danger is not incorrect suggestions. It is ungoverned execution.

If you cannot answer these questions without a meeting, you are not ready:

- What is the system allowed to send to customers?
- Which segments are restricted?
- What approvals are required for pricing, claims, or commitments?
- What triggers escalation?
- What is the rollback path when the system makes a wrong move?

Executives call these "AI risks." They are not. They are architecture decisions.

## How to Locate Your Current Level (Without Lying to Yourself)

Most organizations misclassify themselves. They label Level 1 assistance as Level 3 orchestration because the UI looks sophisticated. Use these four diagnostics instead.

**Diagnostic 1: Who owns the next step?**

- **Level 1**: the rep owns it.
- **Level 2**: the workflow assigns it.
- **Level 3**: the system sequences it across steps and roles.
- **Level 4**: the system executes it unless it hits a boundary.

**Diagnostic 2: Where does "accountability" live?**

- **Level 1**: dashboards and manager oversight (missions, targets, inspection) [https://www.salesscreen.com/blog/sales-autonomy/].
- **Level 2**: workflow compliance (required steps and fields) [https://www.activepieces.com/blog/sales-automation-examples].
- **Level 3**: orchestration metrics (coverage, handoff reliability, follow-through rates) [https://www.highspot.com/blog/sales-workflow-automation/].
- **Level 4**: governance (permissions, audit, reversibility, escalation).

**Diagnostic 3: What breaks when a top rep leaves?**

- **Level 1–2**: deals slip, but workflows still "function."
- **Level 3**: less breaks because orchestration carries continuity.
- **Level 4**: continuity is expected; the system should absorb most of the loss in coordination capacity.

**Diagnostic 4: What do managers actually do?**

- **Level 1**: chase updates and inspect activity.
- **Level 2**: enforce process and clear bottlenecks.
- **Level 3**: manage exceptions and tune plays.
- **Level 4**: govern the system—policies, boundaries, and escalation integrity.

## The Progression Most Leaders Get Wrong

The ladder is not a shopping list. It is a sequence of control redesign.

A common failure pattern looks like this:

- Leaders deploy Assisted Tasks (Level 1) and see local productivity gains.

- They add Guided Workflows (Level 2) and get modest consistency.
- They attempt Autonomous Execution (Level 4) before they have orchestration discipline (Level 3).
- The system creates noise, misfires, or brand drift.
- The organization declares autonomy "too risky" and retreats to manual heroics.

That is not a technology failure. It is a sequencing failure.

TheSalesBlog's autonomy-versus-discipline argument becomes a warning label here: autonomy scales outcomes only when discipline is already institutionalized [https://www.thesalesblog.com/blog/sales-effectiveness-autonomy-vs-discipline].

## What "Next Level" Progress Actually Looks Like

Leaders ask, "How do we move up the ladder?" The correct question is, "What authority can we move into the system without losing control?"

Use this progression:

- **From Level 1 to Level 2**: standardize the path. Reduce improvisation. Embed playbooks into workflows. Do not confuse motivation mechanisms with execution control [https://www.salesscreen.com/blog/sales-autonomy/].
- **From Level 2 to Level 3**: connect workflows into orchestration. Stop optimizing steps in isolation. Build cross-functional flow. Add sequencing, prioritization, and exception packets [https://www.highspot.com/blog/sales-workflow-automation/].
- **From Level 3 to Level 4**: formalize governance. Permission the actions. Instrument audit trails. Define escalation logic. Make rollback real, not theoretical [https://www.onsa.ai/sales-autonomy-ladder].

Activepieces' examples underline the operational truth at Level 2: automation creates value when it prevents manual errors and keeps multi-step motions reliable—but it must be monitored to avoid creating backlogs [https://www.activepieces.com/blog/sales-automation-examples]. That warning does not go away at Level 4. It becomes existential.

## The Inevitable Implication: Autonomy Becomes a Board-Level Operating Capability

Within a few years, "sales execution" will no longer be evaluated primarily as rep performance. It will be evaluated as autonomy maturity. Not because boards love technology. Because boards love predictability.

The autonomy ladder gives you a language for the real work:

- What execution authority belongs to the system?
- What remains human judgment?
- What is governed?
- What is merely automated?

Teams that can answer those questions will scale calmly. Teams that cannot will scale noisily—until noise becomes leakage, and leakage becomes missed quarters.

Chapter 5

# The Agentic Revenue Maturity Model

## The Constraint Is Not Intelligence. It Is Maturity.

Most revenue organizations are not failing to adopt autonomy. They are failing to earn it.

They treat autonomy like a switch: on or off. It is not. Autonomy is a privilege granted by the operating system—when the operating system can contain it.

This is why agentic initiatives keep producing the same two outcomes:

- **Impressive demos** that never become durable production.
- **Production rollouts** that create noise, drift, and governance panic.

The underlying issue is structural. Revenue leaders keep trying to increase autonomy along a single axis—technology—while maturity is multidimensional.

You do not "implement agentic revenue." You redesign the conditions that make governed autonomy possible.

## The Model: Five Dimensions That Determine How Much Autonomy You Can Safely Run

The **Agentic Revenue Maturity Model** measures readiness across five dimensions:

- **Data**: whether the system is anchored to clean, usable truth.
- **Process**: whether execution is consistent enough to orchestrate.
- **Tech Architecture**: whether systems can act end-to-end, not just report.
- **Governance**: whether autonomy is permissioned, auditable, and reversible.
- **Culture**: whether humans trust the system, and the system earns that trust.

Maturity is not "good" or "bad." It is a ceiling on autonomy. If your governance is immature, your autonomy ceiling is low—no matter how modern your tools look. If your data foundation is weak, your orchestration will be noisy—no matter how compelling the agent appears in a pilot.

## The Four Stages of Maturity: A Structural Progression

Every organization will describe itself differently. The pattern underneath is consistent. Agentic revenue maturity progresses in four stages:

### Stage 1: Fragmented Execution

- Multiple definitions of pipeline, qualification, and forecast.
- Process exists, but exceptions run the business.
- Tech stack records activity, then humans stitch reality back together.
- Governance is informal. Permissions are implied.
- Culture relies on heroics and distrusts systems by default.

This is where "AI projects" go to die. Not because the models are weak. Because the organization has not built a governable truth for the models to act on.

### Stage 2: Standardized Control

- Core definitions are declared and enforced.
- Critical workflows are standardized: lead-to-meeting, meeting-to-opportunity, opportunity-to-close.
- Tech stack begins to connect systems into repeatable paths.
- Governance becomes explicit: access, approvals, audit trails.
- Culture shifts from "rep freedom" to "system reliability."

This stage is unglamorous. It is also where most of the leverage begins.

### Stage 3: Orchestrated Execution

- Signals are captured continuously across the revenue chain.
- Work is sequenced across roles and functions without human middleware.
- Architecture supports end-to-end execution, not isolated automations.
- Governance includes exception handling and rollback discipline.

- Culture expects the system to carry baseline coverage, not just assist top performers.

This is where autonomy starts generating structural advantage: less leakage, faster loops, fewer meetings.

**Stage 4: Governed Autonomy**

- The system executes defined plays end-to-end inside permissioned boundaries.
- Humans supervise exceptions, policy, and trade-offs—not routine motion.
- Governance is institutional: approved lanes, monitoring, accountability.
- Culture trusts autonomy because autonomy is constrained, visible, and correctable.

Stage 4 is not "hands-off." It is *hands-on governance* with *hands-off execution.*

## Dimension 1: Data Maturity — From Disputed Records to Actionable Truth

Agentic systems do not tolerate interpretive data. They require executable data. That is the shift.

RevOps maturity frameworks repeatedly converge on the same foundation: until you establish controlled inputs, you cannot scale outputs. Johnny Grow's maturity model frames the progression from laggard to best-in-class as a data-driven roadmap focused on customer insight, efficiency, and personalization—because those capabilities require trusted, unified information flows [https://johnnygrow.com/business-growth/revenue-operations/a-revops-maturity-model/].

### What "mature data" actually means in agentic revenue

- **Semantic clarity**: one definition of qualified pipeline, one definition of stage progression, one definition of "active opportunity."
- **Coverage integrity**: critical fields are populated because the system enforces capture at the moment of execution, not because leadership nags.
- **Lineage**: you can trace why a number is true and where it came from.
- **Latency discipline**: data arrives fast enough to drive action, not just reporting.

### The hidden failure mode: Decision-grade outputs built on non-decision-grade inputs

If your organization still needs a meeting to reconcile pipeline, your data maturity is not "medium." It is operationally unsafe.

Autonomy does not fix disputed truth. It operationalizes it.

## Dimension 2: Process Maturity — From Tribal Motion to Governed Flow

Most revenue leaders confuse process with documentation. Process maturity is not whether you have playbooks. It is whether the playbooks run when humans are tired, distracted, or politically motivated.

RevPartners' RevOps Maturity Model makes the sequencing explicit: progression runs from basic KPI tracking to more advanced forecasting and predictive capability, anchored in evidence-based measurement and leak-fixing rather than aspiration [https://blog.revpartners.io/en/revops-articles/revpartners-revops-maturity-model]. That is exactly the posture agentic revenue requires. You do not "install prediction." You earn it by stabilizing the system it predicts.

### Process maturity markers that matter for autonomy

- **Handoff integrity**: SDR→AE→SE→legal→finance transitions are defined, instrumented, and measurable.
- **Exception design**: the organization knows what "non-standard" looks like and how it's handled.
- **Leak visibility**: dropped follow-ups and stalled deals are detected as system failures, not rep personality issues.
- **Throughput awareness**: routing without capacity planning is just automated backlog.

### The hidden failure mode: Automating chaos makes chaos faster

If your current process maturity depends on heroic sellers, the agent will learn heroics and reproduce them at scale. Then leadership will call it "AI risk." It is not. It is process debt.

## Dimension 3: Tech Architecture Maturity — From Stacks to Execution Fabrics

A modern stack is not an architecture. It is an inventory.

Tech maturity in agentic revenue is the ability to execute end-to-end plays with observable control. That requires an **execution fabric**: systems connected by governed workflows, state awareness, and reliable triggers—not exports, Slack messages, and human memory.

SuperAGI's case studies illustrate what changes when agentic systems are integrated into real execution: examples cite outcomes like a 30% pipeline boost and significant sales augmentation through real-time insights and automation, with readiness assessed via ROI before scaling [https://web.superagi.com/case-studies-how-companies-are-using-agentic-ai-to-boost-conversion-rates-and-reduce-costs/]. Ignore the tool branding. Observe the structural requirement: integration that can carry action, not just analysis.

### Architecture maturity markers

- **Event-driven workflows**: the system reacts to customer behavior and pipeline state changes continuously.
- **State coherence**: "where this account is" has one operational meaning across platforms.
- **Execution observability**: you can see what the system did, why it did it, and what happened afterward.
- **Failure containment**: when something breaks, it breaks locally—not across the revenue machine.

### The hidden failure mode: Integration that appears complete but cannot be governed

If you cannot disable a behavior quickly, you do not have architecture. You have a live experiment.

## Dimension 4: Governance Maturity — "Approved Lanes" or the Autonomy Tax

Governance is not a compliance add-on. It is the operating system of autonomy.

The most useful real-world pattern is not theoretical. It is operational. Andersen Institute describes a logistics firm deploying agentic AI for real-time rerouting while using "approved lanes" with auditable workflows, monitoring, and joint business/IT ownership—reducing delays by 18% and saving $3.2M in penalties [https://andersoninstitute.org/agentic-ai-navigating-roi-challenges/]. That case matters because it demonstrates the correct sequence:

- Define where the agent is allowed to act.
- Make actions observable and auditable.
- Instrument monitoring before scaling autonomy.
- Share ownership across business and IT so governance is not performative.

Revenue leaders should steal the mechanism, not the domain. "Approved lanes" is simply a name for bounded autonomy with explicit control surfaces.

### Governance maturity markers

- **Permissioning**: action classes are scoped (who can send what, change what, commit what).
- **Audit trails**: every action is attributable, reviewable, and explainable.
- **Monitoring**: drift, anomalies, and policy violations are detected early.

- **Rollback**: reversibility is real, tested, and fast.
- **Joint ownership**: governance sits with operators, not just security or IT.

### The hidden failure mode: Governance written as policy but not executed as mechanism

If your governance exists in a document, you do not have governance. You have a false sense of safety. Autonomy will collect that debt with interest.

## Dimension 5: Culture Maturity — Trust Is Not a Feeling. It Is an Outcome.

Culture is the only dimension leaders try to "inspire." That is convenient. It is also wrong.

In agentic revenue, culture follows architecture. Teams trust systems that are:

- predictable,
- constrained,
- auditable,
- and correctable.

Johnny Grow's maturity framing connects capability progression to customer insights, efficiency, and personalization—an implicit cultural shift from siloed effort to system-wide accountability for outcomes [https://johnnygrow.com/business-growth/revenue-operations/a-revops-maturity-model/]. RevPartners similarly emphasizes measurement discipline and sequencing—another cultural shift: away from opinion-led pipeline debates and toward evidence-led operating rhythms [https://blog.revpartners.io/en/revops-articles/revpartners-revops-maturity-model].

### Culture maturity markers

- **Humans supervise** instead of "doing the system's job."
- **Exceptions are valued** because they improve policies and plays.
- **People stop hoarding information** because the system reduces political advantage from private context.
- **RevOps becomes an architecture function**, not a reporting function.

### The hidden failure mode: AI theater

When the org does not trust its own data and process, it treats autonomy like a performance. Pilots become slideware. Dashboards become narratives. Nothing changes downstream.

## Assessment: Locate Your Maturity Without Lying to Yourself

Most maturity assessments fail because they ask teams how they feel. This model is operational. It asks what is true.

**Assessment Question 1: Where does "truth" live?**

- If the answer is "in the CRM, but...," you are Stage 1.
- If the answer is "in governed definitions enforced across systems," you are Stage 2+.

**Assessment Question 2: What percentage of revenue workflows are end-to-end?**

- If humans are still the integration layer, you are Stage 1.
- If workflows are orchestrated across roles with measurable handoffs, you are Stage 3+.

**Assessment Question 3: Can you describe your autonomy boundaries in a single page?**

- If permissions are implicit, autonomy will be unsafe at scale.
- If permissions are explicit by action class, segment, and risk level, you can increase autonomy deliberately.

**Assessment Question 4: What happens when the system makes a mistake?**

- If the answer is "we'll fix it," you do not have rollback.
- If the answer includes containment, audit, and reversal mechanics, you have governable autonomy.

## The High-Leverage Moves: The Few Changes That Unlock the Next Stage

Most transformation programs fail because they attempt to mature everything at once. Maturity does not require broad activity. It requires a few decisive structural moves.

### High-Leverage Move #1: Reduce "Truth Count" to One

One definition of qualified pipeline. One definition of stage progression. One definition of forecast.

This is not a reporting cleanup. It is the foundation for system action. Without it, agents will execute contradictions at machine speed.

### High-Leverage Move #2: Instrument one end-to-end workflow as your "reference circuit"

Pick one workflow that touches multiple functions—opportunity-to-close is the usual choice because it exposes the real friction. Design it as the reference circuit:

- Declared states
- Permissioned actions
- Exception thresholds
- Audit trails
- Rollback paths

This is where architecture stops being a concept and becomes a muscle.

### High-Leverage Move #3: Build "approved lanes" before you build "smart agents"

The logistics case shows the pattern: approved lanes plus auditable workflows plus monitoring preceded scalable autonomy [https://andersennstitute.org/agentic-ai-navigating-roi-challenges/]. Revenue needs the same sequence:

- Approved lanes for customer-facing communication
- Approved lanes for routing and prioritization
- Approved lanes for pricing and terms (narrower, higher governance)

If you cannot name the lanes, you cannot supervise the driving.

### High-Leverage Move #4: Promote RevOps from "reporting" to "control engineering"

RevPartners' maturity model emphasizes analytics progression and evidence-based advancement [https://blog.revpartners.io/en/revops-articles/revpartners-revops-maturity-model]. The operational implication is larger: RevOps becomes responsible for loop integrity—latency, leakage, handoffs, and exception quality. Not just dashboards.

### High-Leverage Move #5: Set an autonomy budget

Autonomy is not a feature rollout. It is a risk allocation decision.

OneReach's Enterprise AI Agent Maturity Model frames maturity as staged progression—moving from automation into advanced coordination—while tying scaling to dashboards, governance, and total cost of ownership discipline, with reported ROI ranges (5x–12x) when sequenced correctly [https://onereach.ai/blog/enterprise-ai-agent-maturity-model-roi-insights/]. The useful takeaway is executive: autonomy must be budgeted.

- How many action classes will we allow the system to execute this quarter?
- How many segments are in-scope?
- What monitoring must exist before expansion?

This turns autonomy from a philosophy into a governable operating plan.

## Sequencing: What Must Be True Before You Turn Up Autonomy

Most organizations ask, "What can agents do?" The correct question is, "What must be true *first*?"

**Before semi-autonomous orchestration (Stage 2 → Stage 3)**

- Definitions are enforced, not negotiated.
- At least one cross-functional workflow is instrumented end-to-end.
- Exception thresholds are designed and measurable.

**Before governed autonomy (Stage 3 → Stage 4)**

- Approved lanes exist for each action class.
- Audit and rollback are tested under pressure, not assumed.
- Monitoring is proactive, not forensic.
- Ownership is joint: business and IT share accountability (as in the Andersen case) [https://andersoninstitute.org/agentic-ai-navigating-roi-challenges/].

### The point of sequencing

Sequencing is not project management. It is risk containment. It prevents the most expensive executive failure in this transition: granting autonomy before you have the mechanisms to govern it.

## The Inevitable Implication: Maturity Becomes the Competitive Differentiator

In the next era, you will not compete on who "uses agents." You will compete on who can *govern* them.

Competitors with higher maturity will run faster loops with less management overhead. They will detect risk earlier. They will execute plays more consistently. They will redeploy human judgment to the moments that actually matter.

Lower-maturity organizations will do what they always do: add tools, add dashboards, add meetings—and call it rigor.

The market will not reward effort. It will reward governable throughput. And governable throughput is a maturity outcome.

# Part II

# The Architecture – Building the Revenue Operating System

Chapter 6

# Redesigning the Revenue Operating System

## Most Revenue Teams Didn't Buy Too Many Tools. They Avoided a Harder Decision.

Tool sprawl is what happens when you try to modernize execution without redesigning the system that governs it. You add capability, but you don't add coherence. You get more "help," but not more control.

This is the moment revenue leaders have to face directly:

- Tools can assist people inside a broken operating model.
- They cannot substitute for an operating system that can execute.

A revenue organization without an operating system is condemned to two recurring behaviors:

- **Documentation** masquerading as management.
- **Meetings** masquerading as coordination.

Agentic revenue does not begin with agents. It begins with *primitives*. The few structural building blocks that make execution safe, governable, and continuously improvable.

## The Shift: From Systems of Record + Dashboards to Systems of Execution + Continuous Optimization

The old architecture optimized for memory. Record what happened. Summarize it. Debate it. Decide what to do next.

That architecture produced a familiar stack: CRM as ledger. BI as scoreboard. Enablement as library.

Modern teams keep the same architecture and bolt on assistance. They call that "transformation." It is not. It is decoration.

The new architecture optimizes for throughput under governance. It treats revenue as a control system: detect → decide → act → learn. Continuously.

Optifai captures the distinction bluntly: systems of record store information; systems of action execute work—automating updates, generating tasks, and turning signal into movement rather than dashboards into debates [https://optif.ai/media/articles/system-of-record-vs-system-of-action/]. That is the structural shift: revenue becomes a system that *does*, not a system that *reports*.

## The Agentic Revenue OS: Four Primitives That Make Autonomy Possible

An "agentic revenue OS" is not a vendor category. It is an operating model with four primitives:

- **Canonical data**
- **Standard objects**
- **Event streams**
- **Feedback loops**

These are not technical preferences. They are the minimum requirements for any system that wants permission to execute on your behalf.

## Primitive #1: Canonical Data — One Truth the System Can Act On

In the dashboard era, "good enough" data was survivable. Humans reconciled. Humans translated. Humans filled in the blanks.

In the execution era, "good enough" becomes operationally dangerous. When systems act, they scale whatever you gave them—truth or fiction.

Canonical data is the enforced source of truth for revenue state. Not "a report." A governed reality with lineage, ownership, and enforcement.

Zuora's revenue automation success stories describe the practical impact when revenue data becomes real-time and execution-grade: organizations using Zuora Revenue and Billing reduced manual processes by 25–75% and gained real-time visibility that supports faster closes and continuous optimization [https://www.zuora.com/guides/revenue-automation-software-buyer-guide/success-stories/]. Read that as architecture, not efficiency: when orders, invoices, and recognition events become canonical, downstream systems can execute instead of wait for reconciliation.

**Canonical data is not "clean data." It is enforceable data.**

- **Defined**: pipeline, stage, qualification, and forecast mean one thing.
- **Current**: state updates at operational cadence, not weekly hygiene.
- **Traceable**: you can explain why the system believes what it believes.

- **Executable**: it is trusted enough to trigger actions.

If your organization has multiple "official" pipeline numbers, you do not have a data problem. You have an operating system problem.

## Primitive #2: Standard Objects — The Shared Language of Revenue Execution

Revenue organizations fail quietly when each function defines the customer differently. Marketing has "accounts." Sales has "opportunities." CS has "health." Finance has "contracts." RevOps has "fields."

Those aren't different perspectives. They are incompatible objects. And incompatible objects create an ungovernable execution environment.

Standard objects are the shared entities the entire revenue system agrees to coordinate around:

- Account
- Buying group / stakeholders
- Opportunity
- Product / package
- Contract / order

- Renewal
- Expansion motion
- Risk state

These objects are not a CRM schema exercise. They are how you prevent parallel automation from producing parallel realities.

Gong's framing of the shift from CRM as a passive system of record to an action-oriented system of action makes the object-level point clear: the system auto-captures interactions, flags risk, and can drive forecast accuracy (including a Piano example cited at 90%) by unifying what "the deal" is across signals, not rep memory [https://www.gong.io/blog/crm-system-of-record-vs-ai-system-of-action]. That only works when the system has stable objects to attach signals and actions to.

### The hidden cost of non-standard objects: humans become translators.

When objects are inconsistent, every forecast meeting contains the same waste: mapping one system's reality onto another. That is not management. That is semantic repair.

## Primitive #3: Event Streams — Revenue Runs on State Change, Not Status Updates

Dashboards are snapshots. Execution requires motion.

An event stream is the continuous flow of state changes that the revenue OS uses to trigger behavior:

- Inbound intent spikes
- Meeting booked / missed
- New stakeholder added
- Proposal sent
- Legal redline introduced
- Discount requested
- Usage threshold crossed
- Invoice delayed
- Renewal window entered

This is not "more data." It is the conversion of reality into triggers.

Zuora's examples again show the structural leap: real-time sales orders and billing events enable automated downstream recognition and operational visibility without waiting for manual cycles [https://www.zuora.com/guides/revenue-automation-software-buyer-guide/success-stories/]. That is event-driven revenue—not quarterly archaeology.

Revenue orchestration platforms describe the value of unified visibility and workflows that automate 40–60% of manual tasks by responding to updates across systems, reducing silos across sales, marketing, and success [https://www.oliv.ai/blog/revenue-orchestration-platform]. The mechanism is the point: execution attaches to events. Not to someone remembering to "update the CRM."

**Event streams collapse latency.**

The old model notices risk in the next meeting. The event-driven model notices risk when it happens. That is how execution becomes a competitive weapon without becoming chaos.

## Primitive #4: Feedback Loops — The System Learns by Operating, Not by Reviewing

Most revenue teams think they have feedback loops because they have QBRs. They do not. They have *postmortems.*

A real feedback loop has four properties:

- **Instrumentation**: the system measures what happened after an action.
- **Attribution**: it knows which play, sequence, or decision produced the outcome.
- **Adjustment**: it changes prioritization or behavior based on results.
- **Propagation**: updates flow into execution automatically, not as "enablement reminders."

Optifai describes this shift in practical terms: automation that not only records but also pre-generates tasks and drafts, using continuous signal (like deal scoring) to drive proactive execution [https://optif.ai/media/articles/system-of-record-vs-system-of-action/]. That is a feedback loop: detect → act → measure → refine.

Gong's system-of-action framing is another representation of the same structure: capture interactions automatically, flag risk, and improve forecast accuracy by turning conversational and deal signals into continuous intervention rather than episodic inspection [https://www.gong.io/blog/crm-system-of-record-vs-ai-system-of-action].

Orchestration platforms explicitly link unified workflows to performance deltas, citing insight-driven execution that can boost win rates (reported ranges of 23–89%) by closing the loop between signal and action instead of leaving insights stranded in dashboards [https://www.oliv.ai/blog/revenue-orchestration-platform]. Whether you accept every number is not the point. The pattern is the point: performance moves when feedback loops are embedded in execution, not in reporting.

## How the Four Primitives Work Together: The Execution Flywheel

Each primitive is insufficient alone. Together, they form an execution flywheel:

- **Canonical data** prevents the system from acting on contradictions.
- **Standard objects** let functions coordinate without translation layers.
- **Event streams** turn reality into triggers with low latency.
- **Feedback loops** turn outcomes into refinement without waiting for management rituals.

This is why "adding an AI layer" fails. Without these primitives, intelligence has nowhere stable to live, and autonomy has nowhere safe to operate. You get suggestions without execution. Or execution without control. Neither is a system.

## The Operational Redesign: Moving From Dashboard Management to System Management

Redesigning the revenue operating system is not a migration project. It is a control project. You are changing what the organization uses as its primary coordination layer.

### Step 1: Declare the canonical truth and make it enforceable

Revenue leaders keep trying to "improve data hygiene." That is the wrong frame. The right frame is: enforce the minimum viable truth required for action.

Default's RevOps framing emphasizes unifying data, process, and technology, reporting outcomes like implementation time cut by 70% and 10 hours/week saved through integrated execution (for example, lead routing) [https://www.default.com/post/what-is-revenue-operations]. Read that as an enforcement story: execution gets faster when truth is unified and routed through a governed path, not reassembled by humans.

### Step 2: Standardize the objects that carry accountability

If sales and finance do not share the same contract object, forecasting will always be a negotiation. If marketing and sales do not share the same account state, pipeline will always be debated. Standard objects are how you remove interpretation from handoffs.

### Step 3: Convert critical workflows into event-driven circuits

Start with one reference circuit you can govern end-to-end:

- Inbound lead → meeting → qualification → opportunity creation
- Or opportunity → proposal → legal → close
- Or renewal window → risk detection → expansion plays

Orchestration platforms describe the advantage of unified visibility and workflows that remove silo drag and automate large portions of manual work [https://www.oliv.ai/blog/revenue-orchestration-platform]. That's what a reference circuit is: one flow that no longer requires human middleware to keep moving.

### Step 4: Install feedback loops where the money leaks

Most revenue leakage is not a sales skill problem. It is an unobserved system failure:

- follow-ups that didn't happen,
- stakeholders that were never mapped,
- procurement friction surfaced too late,
- renewal risk detected after sentiment turned.

Gong's system-of-action approach demonstrates the pattern: continuous capture and risk flagging turns coaching and forecasting from episodic management into ongoing control [https://www.gong.io/blog/crm-system-of-record-vs-ai-system-of-action]. That is where feedback loops pay for themselves: not in prettier reports, but in fewer silent deal deaths.

## What Changes for Leaders: You Stop Managing People as the Primary System

This operating system shift forces a leadership shift. Revenue leaders stop being chief reminder officers. They become designers of governable throughput.

Your new questions are not:

- "Did reps make enough calls?"
- "Did we update Salesforce?"
- "Do we have the right dashboards?"

Your new questions are:

- **Where is canonical truth enforced?**
- **Which objects carry accountability across functions?**
- **Which event streams trigger action without meetings?**
- **Which feedback loops continuously tighten execution?**
- **Where do exceptions escalate, and how cleanly?**

This is how you replace heroic selling with a system that can be trusted to run.

## The Forward Implication: Autonomy Will Not Scale on Top of a Ledger

For twenty years, CRM-centric operating models taught companies to treat revenue as a documentation problem. That habit is now a liability.

Systems of action are not "the next tool category." They are the inevitable successor to systems built for record-keeping. Optifai's distinction makes it plain: recording work and executing work are different architectures, and confusing them is how teams accumulate capability without gaining control [https://optif.ai/media/articles/system-of-record-vs-system-of-action/].

Zuora's automation stories show what happens when canonical data and event-driven execution replace manual revenue workflows: cycle time compresses, manual effort drops materially, and optimization becomes continuous instead of episodic [https://www.zuora.com/guides/revenue-automation-software-buyer-guide/success-stories/].

The winners in the next era will not be the teams with the most AI. They will be the teams with a revenue operating system that can:

- hold one truth,
- coordinate around shared objects,
- react to events in real time,
- and improve itself through embedded feedback loops.

That architecture makes autonomy inevitable. Because it makes autonomy governable.

# Chapter 7

# Human-in-the-Loop Control Architecture

## The Problem Isn't Autonomy. It's Unbounded Authority.

Most executives don't actually fear autonomous systems. They fear not knowing what the system will do next.

That fear is rational. Because most "agent rollouts" are not operating model redesigns. They are permission accidents.

In the old revenue organization, control was crude but clear: humans decided; humans acted; managers inspected. Latency was high, but authority lived in people.

In an agentic revenue system, authority moves into the system. That is the point. And the moment authority moves, the organization needs something it has rarely built in revenue: a real control architecture.

Not a policy document. Not a vendor checklist. A mechanism.

## The Shift: From Human Workflow to Controlled Autonomy

Human-in-the-loop (HITL) is widely misunderstood as "a person approves things." That is amateur governance. It creates bottlenecks, political fights, and a false sense of safety.

Real HITL is a distribution of decision rights. It answers three questions with precision:

- **When does the system decide?**
- **When does a human decide?**
- **How does the system escalate, pause, or get overridden?**

Robotics got this right long before revenue did. In NASA's human-in-the-loop collaboration work, the system runs the fast loop—trajectory tracking—while humans provide higher-level intent and supervision; guardrails exist to prevent collisions even as speed increases [https://ntrs.nasa.gov/api/citations/20240003650/downloads/Human-in-the-loop%20CSM.pdf]. That is the pattern revenue systems must adopt:

- Let machines run the high-frequency execution loop.
- Let humans own intent, boundaries, and exception judgment.
- Instrument guardrails so speed doesn't become damage.

## The HITL Control Blueprint: Two Loops, One Governed Outcome

Every scalable autonomy system separates control into two loops.

### 1) The Inner Loop: Machine-Speed Execution

The inner loop is where latency dies. It handles routine decisions and actions that must occur continuously: follow-ups, routing, sequencing, data capture, play execution, nudges, and task orchestration.

Inner-loop work is not "low value." It is *high frequency*. And high-frequency work is exactly what humans cannot do reliably. Humans do not run continuous control systems. They run shifts.

## 2) The Outer Loop: Human Judgment and Policy Control

The outer loop defines what the inner loop is allowed to do. It owns:

- **Intent**: what the business is trying to achieve (pipeline shape, segment focus, margin protection).
- **Boundaries**: the approved lanes of action by segment, channel, and risk class.
- **Governance**: audit, overrides, escalation logic, and accountability.
- **Exception judgment**: the messy, non-linear trade-offs the system should not decide.

In medical and assistive robotics, this model is explicit: supervised loops, fault-tolerant switching, and remote monitoring are used to manage uncertainty and safety while maintaining operational speed [https://pmc.ncbi.nlm.nih.gov/articles/PMC11157102/]. Revenue has the same need. Not because selling is surgery. Because brand, compliance, pricing, and commitment are irreversible once executed at scale.

## Decision Rights: A Clean Partition of Who Decides What

A workable HITL design starts with explicit decision rights. Not "AI helps reps." Decision rights.

### System-Decides (Default)

These are actions that should execute without human approval because the cost of waiting is higher than the risk of action—*when contained inside guardrails*. Examples:

- Sequence progression based on response events
- Meeting reminders and confirmations
- Data enrichment and field completion with lineage
- Routing decisions inside declared territory and segment rules
- Follow-up creation after a defined no-response window

### Human-Decides (Always)

These are actions where mistakes create strategic, legal, or reputational exposure. They should never be delegated without explicit redesign and board-level appetite. Examples:

- Pricing exceptions outside approved discount corridors
- Non-standard terms, indemnities, or claims
- Customer-facing commitments that create delivery obligations
- Brand-sensitive communications for regulated segments
- Strategic account repositioning (targeting decisions that change posture)

### Shared Decision (Conditional Authority)

This is the real battleground. Shared decision rights are conditional: the system can act until it crosses a boundary, loses confidence, or detects an anomaly. Then it escalates with context, options, and a recommended action.

This is how high-performing HITL systems avoid the two fatal extremes:

- **Automation theater**: humans rubber-stamp everything, turning speed into bureaucracy.

- **Autonomy panic**: the system acts freely until it causes damage, then gets shut down.

Humanloop's approach in content moderation and contract classification is instructive: the system routes only high-uncertainty cases to experts, reducing total human load while preserving accuracy and intent [https://www.uclb.com/case-studies/humans-in-the-loop/]. That is not a tooling idea. It is an operating model principle: humans are reserved for uncertainty, not volume.

## Guardrails: The Mechanisms That Preserve Brand, Compliance, and Intent

Guardrails are not "guidelines." Guardrails are enforced constraints. Without enforcement, you don't have guardrails. You have hopes.

### Guardrail Type 1: Permissioned Action Classes

Define action classes and permission them explicitly:

- Communications (send, draft, queue)
- Routing (reassign, prioritize)
- Record mutation (stage changes, close dates, forecast category)

- Commercial moves (discount suggestions, packaging prompts)

Then bind permissioning to role, segment, and channel. Not everyone gets the same autonomy. Not every account should receive the same autonomy.

### Guardrail Type 2: Policy Constraints (What the System Cannot Violate)

These are non-negotiables the system must check before it acts:

- Regulated-language restrictions by industry/geo
- Approved claims library for outcomes and ROI statements
- Discount corridors and approval thresholds
- Data handling constraints (what data can be used in customer messaging)

The point is not compliance for its own sake. The point is to make intent executable: your strategy becomes constraints the system can enforce at speed.

### Guardrail Type 3: Safe Forecasting (Detect Risk Before It Becomes Damage)

NASA's work highlights a robotics truth revenue leaders should steal: safe forecasting is used to prevent collisions in collaborative environments while maintaining speed [https://ntrs.nasa.gov/api/citations/20240003650/downloads/Human-in-the-loop%20CSM.pdf]. In revenue, "collisions" look like:

- Over-contacting buyers across channels
- Contradictory messages from marketing and sales
- Premature commitments before legal/commercial readiness
- Pipeline manipulation that destabilizes forecasting integrity

Your system must forecast downstream impact, not just execute local optimization. Otherwise, autonomy accelerates your internal contradictions.

## Escalation Design: Exceptions Are Not Failures. They Are the Control Surface.

In a mature autonomous revenue system, exceptions are not embarrassing edge cases. They are the mechanism by which the system stays safe while moving fast.

The design goal is simple:

- Reduce the volume of escalations.
- Increase the quality of escalations.

### Escalation Triggers (When the System Must Stop Acting)

- **Uncertainty**: confidence drops below a threshold (e.g., ambiguous stakeholder role, conflicting signals).
- **Policy conflict**: an action would violate a brand/compliance constraint.
- **Anomaly detection**: unusual deal motion, unusual discounting pattern, abnormal customer responses.
- **Irreversibility**: the action would create a lasting commitment (pricing, terms, claims).

In behavior-assistant robotics, supervised loops and fault-tolerant switching exist precisely for these moments—when uncertainty rises, the system changes mode and escalates control to maintain safety [https://pmc.ncbi.nlm.nih.gov/articles/PMC11157102/]. Revenue needs the same discipline: mode switching is not technical. It is governance executed as design.

## The Exception Packet (What the System Must Provide When It Escalates)

Escalations fail when they arrive as alerts. Alerts create noise. Noise creates disregard.

A real escalation is an exception packet:

- **State**: what is happening now (deal status, stakeholders, timeline).
- **Trigger**: what caused the escalation (policy conflict, anomaly, uncertainty).
- **Options**: 2–3 courses of action, each inside approved lanes.
- **Recommendation**: what the system would do if permitted, with rationale.
- **Risk preview**: what happens if nothing is done.

This is how humans stay in control without becoming the workflow.

## Overrides: The Ability to Stop the System Is the Price of Running It

Autonomy without immediate override is not autonomy. It is exposure.

HITL systems in the real world are built around fallback modes and human takeover. Sogolytics' examples make the point across domains: doctors approve AI-assisted diagnoses, analysts review fraud alerts, and drivers are the fallback layer in autonomy systems [https://www.sogolytics.com/blog/human-in-the-loop-ai/]. The pattern is invariant:

- Routine motion is automated.
- High-risk edge cases are escalated.
- A human can take over when thresholds are crossed.

### Override Types You Must Design

- **Action override**: block a specific message, route, or update before it executes.
- **Play override**: halt an entire sequence or motion across a segment.

- **Policy override**: temporarily tighten or loosen a constraint, with audit trail.
- **Kill switch**: stop all customer-facing actions immediately.

If you don't have these, your organization will build them ad hoc during the first incident. That is the revenue equivalent of designing a fire exit after the fire.

## Approval Flows: Where Human Review Actually Belongs

Approval is not governance. Approval is a specific tool you use sparingly.

Most organizations overuse approvals because they lack better guardrails. They install review gates everywhere and wonder why autonomy "doesn't deliver speed."

A workable model uses approvals only for:

- **Irreversible commitments** (terms, pricing exceptions, binding promises)
- **Regulated claims** (anything that can become discoverable or litigated)
- **Brand risk moments** (public optics, strategic accounts, sensitive contexts)

Everything else should be governed by permissioning, constraints, and audit—so it can execute without permission.

## Exception Handling at Scale: Humans Should See Less, But Understand More

The purpose of HITL is not to "keep humans involved." It is to keep humans effective.

Parseur's real-world case studies show the operational pattern in claims and document processing: AI handles standard extraction, humans handle complex cases; reported outcomes include 70% automation in an insurance claims context and reductions in false positives (reported 67%) when exception handling is designed correctly [https://parseur.com/blog/hitl-case-studies]. That is the revenue translation:

- Let machines clear the routine.
- Let humans resolve the complex.
- Measure the boundary quality relentlessly.

### The Dangerous Failure Mode: "Human-in-the-Loop" as a Blanket Role

If your HITL design says "manager approves agent actions," you built the wrong thing. You built a new meeting. At machine speed.

The correct design is role-specific:

- **Legal** governs specific action classes (terms, claims language).
- **Finance** governs pricing corridors and margin exceptions.
- **Sales leaders** govern account strategy pivots and escalation resolution.
- **RevOps** governs workflow integrity, policy enforcement, and audit.

HITL is not one "human." It is the right human at the right boundary.

## Governance Patterns That Actually Work

### Pattern 1: Approved Lanes

Approved lanes are pre-authorized zones of autonomous action. They are the only way to scale autonomy without scaling risk.

A lane specifies:

- Segment scope
- Action classes allowed
- Policy constraints
- Escalation triggers
- Audit requirements

Inside the lane, the system moves at machine speed. Outside the lane, it escalates.

### Pattern 2: Confidence-Gated Autonomy

Not all decisions deserve the same autonomy. The system should act freely when confidence is high and the action is reversible. It should escalate when confidence drops or impact rises.

Humanloop's approach—routing high-uncertainty cases to experts—captures the essential mechanism [https://www.uclb.com/case-studies/humans-in-the-loop/]. This is how you avoid turning your best people into full-time supervisors.

### Pattern 3: Feedback-Driven Tightening

Guardrails should not be static. They should tighten based on incident patterns and loosen based on demonstrated safety.

Sogolytics emphasizes feedback loops and vigilant monitoring as core HITL practice [https://www.sogolytics.com/blog/human-in-the-loop-ai/]. That matters because the primary governance job is not preventing all mistakes. It is preventing the same mistake from repeating at scale.

## What Changes for Executives: You Govern the System, Not the Queue

Most leadership teams will try to manage agentic execution the way they managed humans: more approvals, more dashboards, more check-ins.

That approach collapses under volume. It turns autonomy into bureaucracy and calls it control.

The executive posture becomes simpler and harder:

- **Define decision rights.**
- **Engineer guardrails as mechanisms.**
- **Design escalation as exception packets, not alerts.**
- **Install overrides and test them under pressure.**
- **Continuously tune boundaries based on evidence.**

This is what it means to preserve brand, compliance, and intent while running faster loops than humans ever could. Not by slowing the system down. By making speed governable.

## The Inevitable Implication: Autonomy Will Be Credited to Those Who Can Contain It

The next revenue leaders will not be defined by how aggressively they automate. They will be defined by how precisely they allocate authority.

Companies that build HITL control architectures will scale autonomy calmly: fast inner loops, disciplined outer loops, clean escalation, real overrides.

Companies that skip control design will oscillate: they will grant autonomy, suffer incidents, then retreat to manual heroics. Not because autonomy failed. Because governance never existed.

In the agentic era, the ability to contain autonomy is the ability to compound it.

# Chapter 8

# From Dashboards to Orchestration Engines

## Dashboards Don't Run Revenue. They Narrate It.

Dashboards were built for a world where the revenue organization had one primary constraint: human attention. You couldn't see everything, so you built screens to summarize what mattered. Then you built meetings to interpret those screens. Then you built follow-ups to make the interpretation real.

That operating model is now structurally misaligned with how revenue actually behaves. Not because dashboards are "bad." Because inspection is an inherently delayed control system.

Dashboards answer the old question: *"Tell me what's happening."*

Modern revenue requires the new question: *"Do something about it now."*

## The Structural Shift: From Observation to Execution

Revenue used to be tolerated as a lagging function. You could afford a weekly readout because buyers moved slower and channels were fewer. Now revenue is a multi-threaded environment: inbound intent, outbound touches, product usage, customer sentiment, procurement constraints, and renewal timing all move simultaneously.

Dashboards do not fail because they lack data. They fail because they lack authority. They create awareness without changing trajectory.

Orchestration engines change the entire operating model. They treat revenue as a control system:

- **Detect** signals continuously.
- **Decide** within declared policies and priorities.
- **Act** across systems and teams.
- **Coordinate** handoffs without human middleware.
- **Escalate** exceptions with context when judgment is required.

This is not "better reporting." It is a different architecture: an execution layer that sits above functions and below leadership—a system that converts signals into coordinated movement.

## Why Inspection Fails as a Control Layer

Inspection-based revenue management breaks in three predictable ways.

### 1) The Latency Tax

By the time a dashboard reflects reality, reality has already moved. The buyer has already formed an opinion. The competitor has already engaged. The internal handoff has already stalled.

Leaders often confuse visibility with control. Visibility is passive. Control requires intervention.

### 2) The Interpretation Bottleneck

Dashboards create a second bottleneck: interpretation. Someone must decide what a metric means, what matters now, and who should act. That decision then has to be translated into tasks across multiple tools and teams.

This is why "rev ops rigor" so often becomes calendar density. The meeting is not collaboration. The meeting is the operating system compensating for the lack of orchestration.

### 3) The Cross-Functional Drift

Dashboards fragment along functional lines. Marketing has engagement analytics. Sales has pipeline. Customer success has health scores. Each view can be locally accurate and globally useless.

Revenue doesn't leak inside functions. It leaks between them. Orchestration engines exist because the boundary is where execution breaks.

## What an Orchestration Engine Actually Is

An orchestration engine is not an analytics layer. It is a governed execution system that:

- treats behavioral and system events as real-time inputs,
- applies decisioning logic to prioritize and sequence work,
- triggers actions across marketing, sales, and customer success,
- prevents contradictory or duplicate motion,
- and coordinates handoffs so the buyer experiences one company, not four departments.

Orchestration is where autonomy becomes operational. And where "AI in revenue" stops being an assistant and becomes capacity.

## The Orchestration Stack: Four Layers Leaders Must Design

If you want orchestration without chaos, you design it in layers.

### Layer 1: Signal Detection (What We Notice)

Signals are events that indicate intent, risk, or opportunity: form submissions, pricing page views, email fatigue, non-response windows, feature adoption, renewal windows. Dashboards aggregate signals. Orchestration engines subscribe to them.

### Layer 2: Decisioning (What We Decide)

Decisioning is where strategy becomes executable. It encodes priorities and constraints:

- Who gets contacted?
- How quickly?
- Through which channel?
- When do we escalate?
- When do we stop?

This is also where governance lives. Because the most dangerous automation is not the wrong email. It is the wrong decision propagated at machine speed.

### Layer 3: Action (What We Do)

Action is not "creating a task." Action is executing within tools: launching a sequence, routing an account, suppressing a send, scheduling a follow-up, generating a briefing, triggering an onboarding step.

### Layer 4: Coordination (How Work Moves Between Teams)

A revenue engine is only as strong as its handoffs. Coordination ensures that marketing actions, sales follow-ups, and CS motions don't collide, duplicate, or undermine each other.

This is the quiet power of orchestration: it turns cross-functional intent into coordinated behavior without meetings as middleware.

## Five Real-World Patterns That Prove the Shift

The most useful evidence is not "AI can do X." It is where orchestration collapses latency, prevents internal conflict, and moves the buyer journey forward automatically. These cases show the operating model change in the wild.

### Case 1: LeanData — GTM Routing as a Real-Time Control System

LeanData describes orchestration workflows where the system detects new website leads as signals, matches and routes them to prevent duplicate outreach, and triggers sales engagement sequences in tools like Outreach or Salesloft—coordinating follow-through across marketing and sales instead of waiting for dashboard review and manual assignment [https://www.leandata.com/blog/sales-engagement-workflows-gtm-orchestration/].

This is not a lead management upgrade. It is a control upgrade.

- **Old world**: marketing reports lead volume; sales later complains about quality; RevOps later tries to reconcile attribution.
- **Orchestrated world**: the signal triggers a governed path immediately—routing, sequencing, de-duplication—so the buyer experiences continuity, not internal hesitation.

The structural point: routing becomes an execution layer, not an administrative chore. You remove the gap where revenue quietly leaks—between "interest happened" and "we reacted."

### Case 2: CSG Xponent — Overcommunication as a Revenue Leak, Fixed by Orchestration

CSG Xponent's journey orchestration example describes agents processing engagement signals with real-time decisioning at high volume (reported as 100 million decisions per day), identifying overcommunication, and triggering optimized sending behavior. The reported outcomes include a 40% reduction in email volume and $2–3M in additional monthly revenue [https://www.cxtoday.com/customer-engagement-platforms/customer-journey-orchestration-features-examples-predictions/].

Most organizations treat overcommunication as a "marketing best practice" problem. It isn't. It's a systems problem: too many teams, too many campaigns, too little coordination.

Dashboards can tell you open rates fell. Orchestration engines prevent the collision before it happens. They do not merely observe fatigue. They suppress it.

The deeper implication: orchestration is not about sending more. It is about sending *less* with higher precision—and protecting trust as a measurable asset.

### Case 3: HeyReach — The 90-Second Gap Between Website Intent and Sales Action

HeyReach outlines an orchestration flow where a HubSpot form submission triggers a webhook; agents pull intelligence (including ICP scoring via tools like Clay), assign the right rep via Slack, and launch personalized outreach in roughly 90 seconds—then extend into discovery preparation and multi-channel workflows without human handoffs [https://www.heyreach.io/blog/sales-orchestration].

This case matters because it reveals where modern revenue teams actually lose deals: not at negotiation, but at response-time and continuity.

- A buyer raises their hand.
- The dashboard updates.
- A meeting is scheduled to discuss "speed to lead."
- Three days later, someone follows up.

That story is common. It is also self-inflicted. Orchestration doesn't "make reps work harder." It eliminates the idle time created by human-timed processes. The 90-second response isn't a tactic. It's a redesigned control loop.

### Case 4: Optimove — Marketing as a Dynamic Execution Calendar, Not a Campaign Factory

Optimove describes campaign orchestration through AI self-optimizing journeys that detect customer actions and orchestrate personalized messaging across channels using a marketing calendar—aligning priorities dynamically rather than measuring results after the fact and manually reconfiguring campaigns [https://www.optimove.com/resources/learning-center/marketing-campaign-orchestration].

The strategic significance is not personalization. It's governance over motion.

Most marketing organizations run campaigns like launches: discrete bursts followed by performance analysis. Orchestration replaces the "launch then learn" rhythm with continuous adjustment inside a controlled framework.

That is how marketing stops being a content producer and becomes an execution partner to revenue: the system can shift cadence, channel, and sequencing based on observed behavior, without waiting for a postmortem.

### Case 5: Braze — Onboarding as an Event-Driven Customer Success System

Braze's automation examples describe event-driven onboarding and engagement flows where integrations (e.g., Segment to Braze) detect user interactions and trigger push notifications, reminders, and drip campaigns with personalized recommendations—improving outcomes such as retailer order frequency [https://www.braze.com/resources/articles/marketing-automation-examples].

Onboarding is where most companies quietly lose expansion. Not because CS teams don't care. Because onboarding is full of micro-events that humans cannot monitor continuously: critical feature adoption, hesitation points, drop-offs, and early signals of misfit.

Dashboards show you activation rates after damage is done. Orchestration intervenes at the moment of deviation:

- the customer stalls,
- the system detects it,
- the right nudge or human outreach is triggered,

- and the customer trajectory is corrected before churn risk crystallizes.

This is where the revenue organization stops ending at "closed-won" and starts operating as a continuous engine across lifecycle.

## The Second-Order Effects Leaders Miss

Teams adopt orchestration thinking they're buying speed. They are actually buying a different set of structural advantages.

### 1) Coordination Becomes a System Property

When orchestration is real, coordination stops being something you beg people to do. It becomes embedded. The system routes, sequences, and suppresses conflicting actions by design.

Your organization stops needing "alignment" as a recurring meeting outcome. It gets alignment as a default operating condition.

### 2) Revenue Becomes Less Dependent on Local Competence

Dashboards reward the best operators because only the best operators can translate insight into action quickly.

Orchestration raises the baseline. Not by making everyone brilliant. By making execution reliable.

### 3) The Buyer Experiences One Company

Most "buyer experience" problems are coordination failures: two messages in two tones from two teams, two conflicting follow-ups, three departments asking for the same information.

Orchestration is how you stop leaking trust through internal fragmentation.

## The Failure Mode: Orchestration Without Discipline Becomes Noise at Speed

Orchestration is not inherently good. It is inherently powerful. And power without constraints produces incidents.

Leaders often trigger the same predictable failure:

- They instrument signals aggressively.
- They automate actions enthusiastically.
- They fail to define suppression rules, priority, and ownership.

The result is machine-generated chaos: duplicate outreach, conflicting plays, escalations as alerts, and teams retreating back to manual control because "automation got messy."

That is not a repudiation of orchestration. It is a sign the operating system wasn't ready to carry authority.

## How to Architect Orchestration Without Losing Control

This is not a tooling decision. It is a design decision. Revenue orchestration needs three architectural commitments.

### Commitment 1: One Signal Taxonomy

If marketing calls it "engaged," sales calls it "warm," and CS calls it "healthy," your orchestration system will coordinate fiction. Define the signal language once. Then enforce it in workflows, not in slides.

### Commitment 2: Suppression and De-duplication as First-Class Design

Orchestration is not only about triggering actions. It is equally about preventing actions.

The CSG example is structurally instructive: identifying overcommunication and reducing send volume was not a side effect; it was the value [https://www.cxtoday.com/customer-engagement-platforms/customer-journey-orchestration-features-examples-predictions/].

If you don't design suppression, you don't have orchestration. You have automated spamming with better analytics.

### Commitment 3: Cross-Functional Plays, Not Functional Automations

Functional automation is "marketing triggers a nurture." Orchestration is "a buyer event triggers a coordinated sequence across marketing, sales, and CS with explicit handoffs and stop conditions."

LeanData's GTM workflow illustrates the cross-functional design principle: detecting signals, routing correctly, preventing duplicates, then coordinating engagement across the GTM stack—so actions don't collide [https://www.leandata.com/blog/sales-engagement-workflows-gtm-orchestration/].

## The Operating Model Outcome: Revenue Moves From Reporting Cadence to Execution Cadence

Dashboards run on reporting cadence: daily, weekly, monthly. Orchestration runs on execution cadence: continuous.

That is the actual divide. It is not "AI versus no AI." It is whether your revenue organization can:

- detect meaningful changes as they occur,
- trigger movement without internal negotiation,
- and keep the buyer journey coherent across functions.

Once a competitor has that architecture, your dashboard advantage becomes cosmetic. You can have the cleanest reporting in the category and still lose on throughput. Because the market doesn't reward awareness. It rewards response.

## The Inevitable Implication: Dashboards Become Secondary. Execution Becomes Primary.

Dashboards won't disappear. They will be demoted. They become the audit layer—useful for oversight, explanation, and governance. Not the steering wheel.

Orchestration engines become the steering wheel. They are where intent becomes behavior. Where signal becomes movement. Where revenue becomes a system that acts, not a team that reacts.

The companies that make this shift will look unnervingly calm. Not because they work less. Because their operating model doesn't require constant human intervention to remain coherent.

Everyone else will keep "reviewing the dashboard." And explaining, with great confidence, why the quarter slipped.

Chapter 9

# Continuous-Verification Forecasting

## The Forecast Meeting Is a Museum Tour

Most revenue forecasting is a ritual built for a slower world. A monthly call. A spreadsheet export. A round of confidence theater. A number that becomes "the forecast" because everyone is tired and the calendar demands closure.

That process does not fail because leaders are careless. It fails because the control loop is structurally wrong.

Forecasting was treated as a *reporting* function. In an agentic revenue system, forecasting becomes a *governance* function.

The shift is simple to name and hard to accept:

- **Old world:** forecasting is a monthly narrative about what already happened.
- **New world:** forecasting is a living system that continuously checks itself against reality and adjusts its commitments.

In competitive revenue environments, the forecast is not a number. It is a pacing mechanism. And pacing mechanisms cannot run on stale inspection cycles.

## The Shift: From "Call Your Number" to Self-Checking Probability

Continuous-verification forecasting replaces opinion with instrumentation. Not because human judgment is irrelevant. Because human judgment belongs in exceptions and trade-offs, not in routine probability maintenance.

A continuously verified forecast has three defining characteristics:

- **It ingests live signals.** The forecast changes when the buyer changes.
- **It re-scores continuously.** Probabilities update as conditions update, not when the calendar updates.
- **It validates itself.** The system monitors drift, error, and regime change as a first-class operating discipline.

This is not a "better forecast template." It is a different operating model: forecasting becomes a closed-loop system.

## What "Live Signals" Actually Means (And Why Most Forecasts Don't Have Them)

Most revenue teams claim they use signals. What they actually use is *fields*—stage, close date, amount, and a rep's confidence score. Those are not signals. Those are declarations.

Live signals are observable evidence that the buyer journey is moving—or stalling—right now:

- **Conversation signals:** stakeholder expansion, decision language, new objections, procurement mentions, competitor references, tone shift.
- **Behavior signals:** meeting attendance patterns, response latency, multi-threading, re-opened proposals, slipped next steps.
- **Product/usage signals:** adoption thresholds, engagement drop-offs, feature activation, admin actions, pilot behavior.

Continuous systems in other forecasting disciplines already treat live feeds as table stakes. In demand forecasting, advanced implementations move into real-time processing and automated alerts for deviations—because waiting for a month to discover demand changed is how you manufacture stockouts and waste [https://themarketingagency.ca/blog/demand-forecasting-case-study/] [https://www.ismworld.org/supply-management-news-and-reports/news-publications/inside-supply-management-magazine/blog/2024/2024-03/optimizing-demand-forecasting-challenges-and-best-practices/].

Revenue leaders should read that as a structural translation: if your forecast cannot consume live buyer evidence, it is not a forecast. It is a lagging explanation.

## The Continuous-Verification Forecast Loop

A continuously verified forecast runs the same loop, relentlessly:

- **Sense**: ingest live signals as events.
- **Score**: update probability and expected value by opportunity and by segment.
- **Verify**: measure forecast quality continuously, detect drift, detect regime change.
- **Intervene**: propose corrective actions and escalate exceptions when risk rises.

- **Learn**: adjust model behavior, thresholds, and playbooks based on outcomes.

Notice what's missing: the calendar. This is not "weekly instead of monthly." It is "always."

## Verification Is the Difference Between Forecasting and Numerology

Most revenue forecasts are evaluated in one crude way: did we hit the number? That is not verification. That is a postmortem.

Continuous-verification forecasting borrows a more mature discipline: you score the forecast *as it runs*. You track quality by condition and by threshold, not just as a single end-of-period miss or hit.

Verification research in weather and probabilistic forecasting formalizes this approach: forecasts are stratified by regimes, evaluated by thresholds, and tracked continuously so performance degradation is visible early, not discovered after failure [https://www.cawcr.gov.au/projects/verification/] [https://www.hereon.de/imperia/md/assets/clm/neu3_t14.pdf].

Revenue has regimes too:

- Enterprise vs. mid-market
- New logo vs. expansion
- Procurement-heavy vs. product-led
- Partner-led vs. direct

A forecast that performs well in one regime and fails in another is not "mostly accurate." It is operationally dangerous because it creates selective blindness. Continuous verification makes that visible while the quarter is still salvageable.

## Agentic Models Don't "Predict the Quarter." They Maintain the Truth

Leaders often ask for a single, definitive forecast number. That is the wrong product. The real product is a continuously maintained belief state about revenue.

Agentic forecasting models do three jobs at machine cadence:

### 1) Continuous Probability Adjustment

When signals change, the system updates close probability and timing. Not because it "has a feeling." Because it observed evidence: the buying group shrank, the security review appeared, the champion went quiet, usage dropped, legal redlines expanded.

Demand forecasting implementations already use machine learning to adjust patterns continuously as new data arrives, with automated alerts when deviations emerge [https://themarketingagency.ca/blog/demand-forecasting-case-study/]. Revenue forecasting is the same game with different signals: live evidence forces probabilistic revision.

### 2) Risk Flagging With Explanation

A risk flag without rationale is an alert. Alerts are noise.

A proper agentic system produces:

- the risk condition,
- the evidence behind it,
- the likely impact on timing and value,
- and the corrective actions most likely to stabilize the deal.

Continuous validation pipelines in machine learning treat drift detection and anomaly flagging as core operational requirements, not "nice-to-haves" [https://encord.com/blog/continuous-validation-machine-learning/]. Revenue forecasting should copy that posture: if the model cannot explain and self-monitor, you cannot trust it to influence commitments.

### 3) Corrective Action Proposals (Not Just Risk Reporting)

The purpose of forecasting is not knowing. It is steering.

A continuously verified forecast proposes interventions:

- add a missing stakeholder,
- trigger an SE deep-dive,
- run a procurement pre-brief,
- escalate executive alignment,
- adjust packaging to protect margin,
- or pull forward a renewal-save play.

This follows the same principle supply chain leaders apply when they incorporate real-time external signals and run regular model reviews: the forecast is only useful if it changes behavior before the outcome is locked in [https://www.ismworld.org/supply-management-news-and-reports/news-publications/inside-supply-management-magazine/blog/2024/2024-03/optimizing-demand-forecasting-challenges-and-best-practices/].

## The Hidden Failure Mode: Continuous Forecasting Without Continuous Verification

Many teams will attempt "real-time forecasting" by refreshing dashboards more frequently. That is not continuous forecasting. That is faster narration.

The real failure mode is subtler:

- Signals stream in.
- Probabilities update.
- Executives start treating the updates as truth.
- No one verifies whether the machine is staying calibrated.

Then drift occurs. Market conditions shift. A new competitor changes buyer behavior. Pricing pressure changes cycle dynamics. Your model becomes confidently wrong—at high frequency.

Continuous validation practice exists precisely to prevent this: monitor performance metrics, detect drift, and retrain or adjust under governance, not under panic [https://encord.com/blog/continuous-validation-machine-learning/].

In revenue terms: verification is not about model hygiene. It is about preventing false certainty from becoming an operating condition.

## The New Managerial Role: From Forecast Judge to System Governor

In the old model, managers were forecast judges. They interrogated reps, negotiated commit categories, and averaged emotion into a number.

In continuous-verification forecasting, managers become governors of a living system. Their job shifts in four ways:

### Role Shift 1: They Govern Signal Quality, Not Rep Optimism

The question stops being, "Do you feel good about this deal?" It becomes, "Is the system receiving the right evidence to maintain a truthful probability?"

Managers enforce instrumentation: stakeholder mapping, next-step integrity, documented constraints, product usage visibility. Not as compliance theater. As forecast stability.

### Role Shift 2: They Tune Thresholds and Escalation Logic

Continuous forecasts require boundaries:

- When does probability change require a human review?
- When does a timing slip trigger exec escalation?
- When does discount behavior signal a margin-risk regime?

Verification disciplines emphasize multi-threshold evaluation because one "accuracy number" hides failure at the edges where real risk lives [https://www.cawcr.gov.au/projects/verification/] [https://www.hereon.de/imperia/md/assets/clm/neu3_t14.pdf]. In revenue, threshold tuning is how you prevent noise while catching the risks that matter.

### Role Shift 3: They Manage Regimes, Not Just Pipelines

A mature forecasting system recognizes regimes and adjusts expectations accordingly. Managers stop treating the pipeline as a single population. They supervise forecast performance by motion type and segment behavior.

When regime performance degrades, managers don't "push reps harder." They call a system issue: signal gaps, play mismatch, routing errors, qualification drift.

### Role Shift 4: They Own the Intervention Queue

Continuous forecasting without intervention is voyeurism.

Managers become the owners of corrective action capacity:

- Which risks deserve human time?
- Which can be handled by system plays?
- Which require cross-functional mobilization?

This is where leadership becomes operationally serious: attention becomes a governed asset, not a meeting outcome.

## A Real-World Analogy Leaders Should Steal: Phased Maturity, Continuous Monitoring

Most executives want continuous forecasting to appear fully formed. It will not. Continuous systems are earned.

Demand forecasting case work shows the familiar maturity progression: earlier phases rely on historical analysis; advanced phases move into real-time data processing, machine learning adjustments, and automated deviation alerts, with ongoing optimization rather than episodic rebuilds [https://themarketingagency.ca/blog/demand-forecasting-case-study/].

That same progression will replay in revenue:

- **Phase 1:** stop lying (canonical definitions, consistent stages, basic forecast hygiene).
- **Phase 2:** instrument signals (conversations, behavior, usage) and integrate event feeds.
- **Phase 3:** run probability maintenance continuously with drift monitoring, exception packets, and corrective plays.

Trying to skip phases produces the predictable executive disappointment: the "AI forecast" becomes impressive in demos and unstable in production. Which is not a forecasting problem. It's a system maturity problem.

## What Changes at the Board Level

Boards will not become more patient because your forecasting system is "in transition." They will become less patient because competitors will tighten their control loops.

Continuous-verification forecasting changes what "forecast quality" means:

- Not just accuracy at quarter-end.
- But stability, calibration, and early-warning power throughout the quarter.

When a board asks, "How confident are you?" the correct answer stops being a single number. It becomes a system claim:

- what the system believes,
- why it believes it,
- how it has verified itself recently,
- and what interventions are already underway.

That is what governance looks like when forecasts are living systems, not monthly ceremonies.

## The Inevitable Implication: Forecasting Becomes a Control System, or It Becomes Decorative

A monthly forecast ritual can survive inside a human-coordinated revenue organization. It cannot survive inside an agentic one.

Once execution accelerates—signals, actions, handoffs—your forecasting must match the cadence of reality or it becomes a lagging story about why you were surprised.

Continuous-verification forecasting is not about getting "the number" right. It is about maintaining a governable truth as reality moves. That truth is what allows leadership to allocate attention, protect margin, and intervene early—without relying on heroics.

In the next revenue era, forecasting will divide leaders into two camps:

- Those who run revenue on continuous truth and controlled intervention.
- Those who hold meetings to re-negotiate reality after it has already changed.

One of those is a system. The other is a tradition.

Do you want to stay ahead of the wave?

The Agentic Revenue Brief

by Tim Cortinovis

How revenue leaders build autonomous execution engines — before their competitors do

Weekly clarity for **CROs, VPs Sales,** and **RevOps** leaders under pressure to deliver growth without adding headcount.

**Get the free Friday Brief**

**https://www.timcortinovis.com/tarb**

High-signal insights on autonomous revenue systems. No hype. No vendor fluff.

Your pipeline looks busy. Your forecast feels fragile. Your reps are drowning in tools.

AI is everywhere. Clarity is not.

Chapter 10

# Intelligent Risk Detection and Pipeline Defense

## The Pipeline Doesn't "Slip." It Degrades.

Revenue leaders still talk about pipeline risk as if it arrives like weather. A bad week. A deal "suddenly" goes dark. A procurement surprise. A competitor appears out of nowhere.

That story is comforting. It's also false. Pipeline risk is rarely a surprise. It is a slow structural degradation that becomes visible only when it is expensive to reverse.

In the manual era, risk management was an artisanal practice. Managers inspected pipelines, interrogated reps, and tried to catch problems in time. The best leaders developed instincts. The rest developed rituals.

In the agentic era, that model becomes non-functional. Not because managers got worse. Because the signal surface area exploded and the response window collapsed.

The shift is decisive:

- **Old world:** risk detection is a manager's intuition applied episodically.
- **New world:** risk detection is a system capability running continuously.

## The Structural Shift: From "Pipeline Review" to "Pipeline Defense"

A pipeline review is an inspection ceremony. It listens for problems.

Pipeline defense is a control architecture. It prevents problems from compounding.

The difference is not philosophical. It is mechanical. Inspection assumes risk is discoverable on a weekly cadence. Defense assumes risk is emergent, multi-signal, and time-sensitive.

That means the unit of management changes. You stop managing deals as narratives. You manage deals as *states*, with continuous verification and intervention.

## What Autonomous Systems See Earlier Than Humans

Humans are good at judgment under ambiguity. They are terrible at continuous detection across thousands of micro-signals.

Autonomous systems win on three categories of early warning—because they don't get tired, they don't privilege loud reps, and they don't need the meeting to notice.

### 1) Stalled Momentum (The Drift Nobody Owns)

Stall is not "no activity." Stall is *loss of forward motion* relative to what the deal requires at this stage.

Typical drift patterns:

- Next step exists, but the buyer didn't schedule it.
- Meetings happen, but no new stakeholders appear.
- Follow-ups occur, but response latency increases each cycle.
- Close dates move, but the underlying dependencies don't.

Managers detect this late because stall hides inside "busy." Autonomous systems detect it early because they track state transitions, not calendar promises.

### 2) Conflicting Signals (The Deal Looks Healthy Because Your Systems Disagree)

Conflicting signals are the most dangerous pipeline condition because they create false reassurance. The rep says "strong champion," but the buying group shrank. Marketing engagement spikes, but the security questionnaire arrived. Product usage rises, but procurement language hardens.

Humans tend to resolve conflict by choosing the most convenient narrative. Autonomous systems can hold contradiction without resolving it—and escalate it as risk.

### 3) Pricing Anomalies and Commercial Distortion (Where Margin Leaks Quietly)

The modern discount is rarely a single event. It's a pattern: price anchoring shifts, concessions stack, terms widen, and the deal remains "on track" until margin has already been traded away.

Autonomous systems can detect the pattern as soon as it starts—because they see corridor violations, timing anomalies, and comparative precedent across the full book, not just inside one manager's span of control.

### 4) Buying Committee Change (The Invisible Org Chart)

Buying committees don't announce that they've changed. They simply stop showing up. Or a new voice appears late with veto power. Or a champion remains, but loses internal leverage.

Humans usually notice when a deal fails. Autonomous systems notice when stakeholder topology changes. That is earlier, and it is salvageable.

## The Reference Pattern: Risk Management as Triage, Not Debate

High-performing risk systems don't produce more alerts. They produce *triage*. They answer, continuously:

- What is normal?
- What is anomalous?
- What is urgent?
- What is irreversible?
- What can be handled by the system vs. what requires human judgment?

Other high-stakes domains already solved this operationally. Not with better meetings. With better pipelines.

## Five Real-World Stories Leaders Should Steal From

### Story 1: Defense Operations — Risk Detection Stops Being a Person's Job

Dash Technologies built an AI-driven platform to automate Safety Data Sheets (SDS) processing for a leading defense organization, increasing processing speed by 65% and cutting manual work by 80% [https://dashtechinc.com/works/ai-risk-reduction-defense-operations/].

Most executives read that as "efficiency." The structural lesson is different: SDS processing is a risk classification problem at scale. The work is not filling out forms. The work is detecting hazardous patterns and inconsistencies fast enough to prevent downstream exposure.

The platform performs what revenue organizations rarely formalize:

- **Automated validation** of incoming information.
- **Risk scoring** based on patterns humans would miss.

- **Exception routing** for human review where the risk is ambiguous or high impact.

That is pipeline defense in its pure form: risk is a system capability, not a manager's heroism. Revenue needs the same upgrade. Not to "save time," but to stop relying on individual vigilance as the primary control layer.

### Story 2: Cybersecurity — Autonomous Testing Finds the Breach Before the Audit Begins

Alias Robotics' CAI (Contextual AI) platform demonstrates autonomous vulnerability discovery across industrial robots and infrastructure, including a case where it discovered CVE-2025-24893 and developed a working exploit in roughly six minutes [https://aliasrobotics.com/case-studies-robot-cybersecurity.php].

The point is not speed for its own sake. It's what speed enables: you find systemic weakness before it becomes an incident.

Revenue has an equivalent vulnerability surface:

- Handoff gaps that allow deals to stall.
- Procurement triggers that appear late without preparation.

- Discounting behaviors that normalize margin erosion.
- Multi-threading failures where one stakeholder quietly controls the outcome.

Traditional pipeline audits are the forecasting equivalent of annual penetration testing. Comforting. Late. Politically optimized.

Pipeline defense requires continuous autonomous "testing" of deal integrity: probing for missing stakeholders, contradictory signals, stage/behavior mismatches, and timing slips that indicate structural weakness—then escalating while recovery is still cheap.

### Story 3: Intelligent Data Pipelines — Reduce Noise, Preserve Visibility, Intervene Earlier

EdgeDelta describes intelligent pipeline security using dynamic filtering, normalization, and AI-powered pattern detection at the edge, achieving 90% data reduction while maintaining visibility and detecting suspicious patterns without overwhelming downstream tools [https://edgedelta.com/company/blog/ai-ready-security-starts-with-intelligent-pipelines].

Revenue organizations have the same unsolved problem: signal overload. Most "risk programs" fail because they produce more flags than the organization can govern. The outcome is predictable: teams stop trusting the system, then revert to opinion.

EdgeDelta's structural contribution is an operating principle:

- **Defense is not more data.** Defense is the right data, shaped in the right place, routed to the right response mode.

Pipeline defense needs an equivalent "edge layer" that:

- Normalizes events across systems (CRM, email, meetings, product usage, proposals, legal).
- Filters low-signal noise aggressively.
- Routes only decision-grade exceptions to humans.
- Maintains visibility so suppression doesn't become blindness.

The goal is not a noisier risk dashboard. The goal is a quieter organization with earlier intervention.

### Story 4: Financial Services Fraud — Triage Beats Raw Detection

SuperAGI cites fraud detection examples including IBM Watson Financial Services and SAS Fraud

Detection, reporting reduced false positives (up to 50% in IBM Watson examples; 25% in SAS examples) and improved detection, with fraud-loss prevention cited up to 30% [https://web.superagi.com/case-studies-in-autonomous-ai-real-world-applications-and-lessons-learned-in-2025/].

It's tempting to focus on the fraud numbers. Ignore them. Steal the architecture.

Fraud systems live or die on one design constraint: they must catch real risk without drowning analysts in false positives. Revenue is the same. If every deal is "at risk," no deal is at risk. You don't have defense. You have anxiety.

Fraud systems formalize three mechanisms revenue leaders need:

- **Anomaly detection** based on comparative precedent (pricing, behavior, timing).
- **Risk scoring** to prioritize attention as a scarce asset.
- **Intervention routing** that determines what gets handled automatically vs. escalated.

This is how risk becomes governable. Not by "more inspection," but by controlled prioritization.

### Story 5: DevSecOps Threat Intelligence — Rollback Is a First-Class Revenue Capability

we45 describes continuous threat intelligence (CTI) embedded in DevSecOps pipelines at a global cloud services provider: detecting vulnerable third-party libraries and supply chain risks pre-deployment, automatically flagging anomalies and triggering remediation such as rollback and quarantine [https://www.we45.com/post/continuous-threat-intelligence-in-devsecops-pipelines].

Revenue leaders should translate this literally:

- **Detection** inside the pipeline, not after the release.
- **Triage** based on severity and exploitability.
- **Playbooks** that trigger remediation automatically.
- **Rollback** that is immediate, not a hero project.

Revenue needs rollback. Not just for systems, but for motions:

- Stop a sequence that is causing buyer fatigue.
- Withdraw a discount suggestion that violates corridor policy.

- Suppress outbound to accounts in active procurement.
- Quarantine a deal from commit status when evidence degrades.

If your only rollback mechanism is "we'll tell the team to stop," you don't have control. You have hope and Slack.

## The Pipeline Defense Framework: Detect → Triage → Score → Intervene → Learn

Pipeline defense is a closed-loop system. It runs continuously and stays auditable.

### 1) Automated Detection: Identify Risk States, Not Just Bad Outcomes

Detection is not "alert me if no activity for 14 days." That is a crude proxy.

Real detection watches for state divergence:

- **Stage-behavior mismatch:** late-stage deal, early-stage evidence.
- **Momentum decay:** cycle time per step increasing, response latency rising.

- **Signal contradiction:** expansion language combined with procurement hardening.
- **Commercial distortion:** discount stacking, term creep, unusual approval patterns.
- **Stakeholder instability:** champion silence, new veto entrants, committee contraction.

This is where autonomous systems outperform humans: they can compute divergence across thousands of opportunities without privileging charisma or hope.

### 2) Automated Triage: Reduce the Surface Area Humans Must Supervise

Triage is the difference between an effective risk system and another notification channel. EdgeDelta's emphasis on filtering and normalization to prevent downstream overload is the correct pattern: reduce noise while maintaining visibility [https://edgedelta.com/company/blog/ai-ready-security-starts-with-intelligent-pipelines].

In revenue terms, triage sorts exceptions into three lanes:

- **Auto-resolve:** the system can take a reversible corrective action (e.g., schedule follow-up, trigger enablement, request stakeholder mapping).

- **Auto-stabilize:** the system can slow or suppress risky motion (e.g., pause outbound, halt multi-channel touches, prevent stage advancement).
- **Escalate:** the system assembles an exception packet for human judgment.

### 3) Risk Scoring: Attention Becomes a Governed Asset

Risk scoring is not a vanity number. It is a queueing system for scarce cognitive bandwidth. Fraud detection's value is inseparable from reduced false positives because it protects analyst attention [https://web.superagi.com/case-studies-in-autonomous-ai-real-world-applications-and-lessons-learned-in-2025/].

A usable revenue risk score must be:

- **Comparable** across deals (so you can prioritize).
- **Decomposable** into drivers (so you can act).
- **Bounded** by governance (so it doesn't rewrite policy).

If leaders can't explain why a deal is "high risk," they won't trust the score. If they don't trust it, they won't act early. Then they'll act late, loudly, and inefficiently.

### 4) Intervention Playbooks: Risk Detection Without Response Is Surveillance

Detection that doesn't trigger action is not defense. It's diagnostics. Useful, but incomplete.

DevSecOps CTI pipelines demonstrate the mature posture: detect, prioritize, then trigger rollback or quarantine before deployment risk crystallizes [https://www.we45.com/post/continuous-threat-intelligence-in-devsecops-pipelines].

Revenue intervention playbooks should be designed the same way:

- **Momentum Recovery**: re-sequence next steps; trigger executive outreach; insert SE support; propose a mutual action plan.
- **Stakeholder Repair**: detect missing roles; prompt mapping; initiate multi-threading actions; escalate for sponsor strategy.
- **Procurement Preemption**: detect legal/procurement language; trigger pre-brief; route contract packet; enforce term corridors.

- **Pricing Defense**: flag corridor violations; require approval; propose package alternatives; stop concession stacking by default.
- **Message Suppression**: pause outbound when buyers show fatigue; prevent multiple departments from contacting simultaneously.

The playbook is the point. Not the alert. Alerts create meetings. Playbooks create outcomes.

### 5) Learning: Prevent the Same Failure From Repeating at Scale

Every incident should tighten the system. Otherwise you are not building defense; you are collecting stories.

The mature model is: when interventions succeed or fail, thresholds and playbooks adjust. Over time, the system escalates less often, but with higher quality. Pipeline defense becomes quieter as it becomes stronger.

## Hidden Failure Modes Leaders Create Themselves

### Failure Mode 1: Risk Inflation

If everything is a risk, nothing is. Risk inflation is what happens when you deploy detection without triage.

You get a flood of "at risk" tags that the organization learns to ignore.

### Failure Mode 2: False Precision

A risk score with two decimals creates the illusion of certainty. The right output is not precision. It is prioritization with explainability.

### Failure Mode 3: Intervention Without Governance

If the system can intervene but you cannot audit, pause, and override, you didn't build defense. You built exposure.

The DevSecOps case makes the mature posture obvious: automatic remediation exists because rollback exists [https://www.we45.com/post/continuous-threat-intelligence-in-devsecops-pipelines]. Revenue needs the same discipline: interventions must be reversible, permissioned, and supervised.

## What This Changes for the CEO, CRO, and Board

Pipeline defense is not a RevOps improvement. It is a change in how the firm governs revenue commitments.

When autonomous risk detection is real:

- Forecast confidence stops being a charisma contest.
- Commit becomes an evidence-backed state, not a rep declaration.
- Margin protection becomes enforceable, not aspirational.
- Deal rescue becomes earlier, smaller, and cheaper.

This is why the shift is inevitable. As soon as one competitor can see and intervene earlier—consistently—everyone else is operating blind by comparison. Not because they lack data. Because they lack a defense system.

## The Inevitable Implication: Risk Management Moves From Talent to Architecture

In the heroic era, a great manager could save a quarter through instinct and escalation. That model does not scale, and it does not survive speed.

In the agentic era, risk management becomes an operating capability: continuous detection, triage, scoring, playbooks, rollback.

Executives who keep treating risk as intuition will hire more "strong managers" and wonder why performance still swings. Executives who treat risk as architecture will build calmer quarters—and a pipeline that resists degradation by default.

Chapter 11

# Automated Growth: Cross-Sell, Upsell, and Expansion

## Most Companies Treat Expansion as a Sales Motion. It's a Systems Motion.

Cross-sell and upsell have been framed as "good account management." Which is another way of saying: fragile, personality-dependent, and inconsistently executed.

The problem is not that teams don't know expansion matters. The problem is that expansion has been run as an *episodic* activity inside a *continuous* customer lifecycle.

Revenue leaders keep trying to fix this with training, SPIFFs, and "QBR rigor." That's not expansion strategy. That's motivational debt.

The structural shift is clean:

- **Old world:** humans notice opportunity, then decide whether to act.
- **New world:** the system maintains a live expansion map, triggers plays, and escalates high-trust moments to humans.

Automated growth is not about sending more offers. It's about running an expansion control loop without flooding the customer, contradicting the brand, or wasting human time on low-probability noise.

## The Expansion Control Loop: Detect → Decide → Orchestrate → Escalate → Learn

Expansion becomes predictable when it becomes a closed-loop system. Not a quarterly hope.

### 1) Detect: Expansion Runs on Intent Signals, Not Rep Intuition

The raw material of automated growth is not "customer information." It is **behavioral evidence**. Signals that indicate readiness, friction, or appetite.

JP Morgan Chase operationalized this directly: AI analyzes transaction data, credit scores, and behavioral patterns to surface cross-sell and upsell opportunities, reporting a 35% increase in cross-sell revenue by using tailored, real-time triggers rather than generic outreach [https://web.superagi.com/case-study-how-companies-are-using-ai-to-identify-upsell-and-cross-sell-opportunities-in-2025/].

The structural lesson is not finance-specific. It's architectural: expansion opportunity is detectable earlier than a human CRM update—if the system is designed to watch.

### 2) Decide: Expand is a Policy Decision, Not a Seller Decision

Most companies let individual roles decide when to push expansion. That creates two predictable outcomes:

- **Under-selling** when humans are busy, cautious, or unaware.
- **Over-selling** when humans are incented, anxious, or indiscriminate.

An agentic revenue system moves "should we offer something?" into a governed decision layer:

- Which signals qualify as expansion readiness?
- Which offers are allowed for which segments?
- What are the suppression rules to prevent fatigue?
- What is the escalation threshold for human involvement?

This is how you scale growth without scaling brand damage.

### 3) Orchestrate: Timeliness Beats Persuasion

Expansion is often won or lost on timing, not messaging. The customer isn't "unconvinced." They're not in the right moment.

Amazon's recommendation system is the canonical example of turning timing into revenue: machine learning uses purchase patterns and browsing behavior to surface "frequently bought together" prompts and upsells, with cross-sells reported as driving 35% of revenue [https://www.allconsultingfirms.com/blog/roi-cross-selling-case-studies/] [https://blog.bismart.com/en/the-most-successful-cases-of-cross-selling-and-up-selling].

The deeper point: when the offer is bound to the moment, it stops feeling like selling. It feels like completion. That is what orchestration accomplishes at scale.

### 4) Escalate: Humans Should Close Trust, Not Chase Timing

Expansion has two fundamentally different categories:

- **Low-trust expansions**: add-ons, bundles, upgrades that are reversible and easily understood.

- **High-trust expansions**: multi-team rollouts, contract complexity, meaningful commercial commitment, strategic re-scoping.

The system should handle the first category with governed automation. The second category should be escalated as a *packaged opportunity* to a human who can build trust and negotiate trade-offs.

TaskUs shows the model: through DemandFarm's account planning system, it streamlined account planning and identified cross-sell/upsell opportunities, reporting 30% upsell and 20% cross-sell increases—while the meaningful expansions still require human-led account work to land well [https://www.demandfarm.com/case-studies/taskus-registered-a-30-increase-in-up-selling-20-increase-in-cross-selling-with-demandfarm/].

### 5) Learn: Prevent the Same Missed Expansion From Repeating

Most expansion programs "review results." A mature system improves itself.

If a pattern shows that a certain signal precedes expansion acceptance, the system increases weighting and routes faster. If a pattern shows fatigue or rejection, suppression tightens automatically. This is not optimization. This is institutional memory—without the hero rep.

## Five Stories That Show Automated Growth Is Already Here

These are not tool demonstrations. They are operating model proofs: detecting intent, acting at the right time, and using humans where trust is earned.

### Story 1: JP Morgan Chase — Cross-Sell as Real-Time Signal Response

JP Morgan Chase used AI to analyze transaction behavior, credit scores, and customer patterns to surface personalized product recommendations, reporting a 35% increase in cross-sell revenue [https://web.superagi.com/case-study-how-companies-are-using-ai-to-identify-upsell-and-cross-sell-opportunities-in-2025/].

This works because it changes the mechanics:

- Signals are continuous, not quarterly.
- Offers are triggered by evidence, not calendar.
- Personalization is not creative—it's routing logic with constraints.

In revenue terms: your expansion motion becomes *state-based*, not rep-based.

### Story 2: Amazon — The Expansion Engine That Doesn't Feel Like Selling

Amazon's cross-sell engine is not famous because it suggests products. It's famous because it makes expansion invisible. It appears as relevance, not outreach.

Case summaries report that cross-sells drive ~35% of Amazon revenue via data-driven recommendations like "frequently bought together," using purchase and browsing patterns [https://www.allconsultingfirms.com/blog/roi-cross-selling-case-studies/] [https://blog.bismart.com/en/the-most-successful-cases-of-cross-selling-and-up-selling].

The structural lesson for B2B is uncomfortable: expansion is often lost because you force the customer to translate value into next steps. A system that suggests the next logical step at the right moment reduces cognitive load. Less persuasion. More inevitability.

### Story 3: TaskUs — Key Accounts as a Managed Expansion Portfolio

TaskUs used DemandFarm to streamline account planning and identify upsell/cross-sell opportunities, reporting a 30% upsell and 20% cross-sell increase [https://www.demandfarm.com/case-studies/taskus-registered-a-30-increase-in-up-selling-20-increase-in-cross-selling-with-demandfarm/].

This matters because it reframes key account growth:

- Not "growth depends on the account owner seeing it."
- But "growth depends on the system surfacing it consistently."

Humans still do the political work. But they stop being responsible for detection. That is how you scale key account performance without requiring a bench of rare talent.

### Story 4: Tushy — Post-Purchase Sequencing Without Flooding

Tushy's post-purchase automation used sequential offers (up to three if declined) and relevant bundling, reporting $191,786 in boosted revenue and 174,022%

ROI [https://www.allconsultingfirms.com/blog/roi-cross-selling-case-studies/].

The mechanism is the story:

- Offer timing is tied to the purchase event.
- Declines change the sequence instead of triggering more noise.
- Expansion becomes a controlled flow, not a one-shot pitch.

This is the overlooked discipline in automated growth: **non-intrusive persistence**. Most companies either spam or go silent. Sequencing is what makes automation feel measured instead of desperate.

### Story 5: HGS — Blended Upsell Agents With Human Closing Power

HGS reports a financial services client using analytics combined with agent upselling to prioritize offers, tripling revenue expectations and generating $50M in additional sales [https://hgs.com/case-studies/combination-of-upselling-and-analytics-yields-50m-dollars-in-additional-sales/].

The key phrase is "combined." This is not a bot closing enterprise expansions. This is the correct division of labor:

- The system detects, prioritizes, and routes.
- Humans close where trust and nuance determine outcome.

This is also why automated growth becomes a margin strategy. Humans get reserved for high-value, high-trust work—not consumed by scanning accounts for weak signals.

## Lifecycle Orchestration: Where Expansion Actually Comes From

Expansion is not a "customer success initiative." It is a lifecycle property. And lifecycle properties are built by orchestration.

### Moment 1: Post-Purchase Completion (Bundling)

This is the cleanest expansion zone: the buyer has already decided. You're not convincing; you're completing. Tushy's sequential post-purchase funnel shows how material this can be when sequencing is controlled and responsive to declines [https://www.allconsultingfirms.com/blog/roi-cross-selling-case-studies/].

### Moment 2: Usage Threshold Crossings (Value Realization)

Usage is the most honest signal. When usage increases, your product is becoming embedded. When usage plateaus, your expansion posture should shift from offer to enablement.

This is where platforms like Amazon win: recommendations are downstream of observed behavior, not upstream of hope [https://www.allconsultingfirms.com/blog/roi-cross-selling-case-studies/].

### Moment 3: Renewal Windows (Risk + Opportunity Converge)

Renewal is where most companies discover they were late. An agentic system should treat renewal windows as dual-purpose:

- **Defense** (detect risk, stabilize usage, resolve dissatisfaction early).
- **Expansion** (upgrade package, extend term, broaden footprint when health is strong).

TaskUs' account planning example highlights this portfolio posture: the system surfaces expansion opportunities while humans handle relationship and complexity [https://www.demandfarm.com/case-studies/taskus-registered-a-30-increase-in-up-selling-20-increase-in-cross-selling-with-demandfarm/].

## The Flooding Problem: Automated Growth Dies by Over-Contact

Most expansion automation fails for a simple reason: it mistakes "more triggering" for "more growth."

A system that can act at machine speed will happily act at machine speed. Unless you engineer restraint.

### The Suppression Stack (What a Mature System Prevents)

- **Channel collision:** marketing and sales touching the same account with different messages in the same 24 hours.
- **Offer duplication:** multiple agents suggesting similar upgrades because each sees partial context.
- **Fatigue escalation:** declines triggering louder attempts instead of smarter sequencing.
- **Premature monetization:** upsell triggered before value realization signals exist.

Amazon and Tushy illustrate opposite ends of the same discipline: expansion works when timing is correct and persistence is sequenced—not when volume is increased [https://www.allconsultingfirms.com/blog/roi-cross-selling-case-studies/] [https://blog.bismart.com/en/the-most-successful-cases-of-cross-selling-and-up-selling].

## Where Humans Must Step In (And Why Most Teams Get It Wrong)

The mistake companies make is binary thinking: either "automate everything" or "keep humans in control." Both are failures.

Humans are not the approval layer. Humans are the trust layer.

### Humans Own Three Expansion Moments

- **Strategic trade-offs:** packaging changes, multi-year terms, scope adjustments, delivery commitments.
- **Political buying groups:** where internal alignment is the real product.

- **High-stakes recovery:** when risk and expansion intersect and the account needs credibility, not sequences.

### The Correct Handoff: From Alert to Expansion Packet

A human should not receive "Upsell opportunity detected." That's noise.

They should receive an expansion packet:

- what the customer did,
- what changed in usage or behavior,
- what they likely need next,
- what has been offered already (and declined),
- what not to do (suppression constraints),
- and the recommended human move.

TaskUs and HGS reflect this blended model implicitly: systems surface and prioritize opportunities; humans land them where relationship and complexity decide outcome [https://www.demandfarm.com/case-studies/taskus-registered-a-30-increase-in-up-selling-20-increase-in-cross-selling-with-demandfarm/] [https://hgs.com/case-studies/combination-of-upselling-and-analytics-yields-50m-dollars-in-additional-sales/].

## The Operating Model Shift: Expansion Becomes a Governed System, Not a Quarterly Campaign

Automated growth is not "AI selling." It is lifecycle orchestration with decision rights.

When you run it correctly, three things become true:

- **Opportunity detection stops being scarce.** Signals are continuously monitored.
- **Customer trust stops being collateral damage.** Suppression and sequencing prevent flooding.
- **Human time stops being burned on scanning.** Humans close trust-heavy expansions and handle exceptions.

The data points from the case record are useful precisely because they're not subtle: 35% cross-sell lifts at JP Morgan Chase, cross-sell contribution reported at 35% of Amazon revenue, meaningful upsell/cross-sell increases at TaskUs, enormous post-purchase ROI for Tushy, and $50M additional sales in the HGS example [https://web.superagi.com/case-study-how-companies-are-using-ai-to-identify-upsell-and-cross-sell-opportunities-in-2025/] [https://www.allconsultingfirms.com/blog/roi-cross-selling-case-studies/] [https://blog.bismart.com/en/the-most-successful-cases-of-cross-selling-and-up-selling] [https://www.demandfarm.com/case-studies/taskus-registered-a-30-increase-in-up-selling-20-increase-in-cross-selling-with-demandfarm/] [https://hgs.com/case-studies/combination-of-upselling-and-analytics-yields-50m-dollars-in-additional-sales/].

These aren't "wins from automation." They are wins from *systemized intent.*

## The Inevitable Implication: Growth Will Be Credited to Whoever Owns the Lifecycle Control Loop

In the next revenue era, the primary growth question stops being: "Can our team upsell?"

It becomes: "Does our system know when the customer is ready, what to offer, what to suppress, and when to hand the moment to a human?"

Companies that answer that question structurally will compound expansion without compounding noise. Everyone else will keep treating cross-sell as initiative-driven revenue—and wonder why it spikes in good quarters and disappears in hard ones.

Chapter 12

# Designing Execution That Closes Its Own Gaps

## The Real Problem Isn't Lost Deals. It's Repeatable Loss.

Every revenue organization loses deals. That's not the failure.

The failure is losing the *same* deal—again and again—under different account names. Same objection. Same stall point. Same handoff breakdown. Same discount spiral. Same "we'll follow up" that never becomes a next step.

Most teams call this "the market." It isn't. It's the operating model.

In the manual era, closing gaps meant leadership attention: pipeline inspection, deal postmortems, enablement sessions, new playbooks, renewed pressure. The system did not improve itself. It waited to be improved.

An agentic revenue system cannot run that way. When execution accelerates, human-led gap closure becomes the bottleneck. You either build a revenue engine that learns from misses automatically, or you accept compounding leakage as a permanent tax.

## The Shift: From Revenue Management to Revenue Control Systems

Most organizations still run revenue like a craft. They rely on individual judgment, tribal fixes, and periodic "alignment."

A control system is different. It has one job: maintain desired performance under changing conditions.

That requires four capabilities that most revenue orgs do not explicitly design:

- **Capture failure signals** without waiting for someone to write a recap.
- **Detect patterns** across failures, not just inside anecdotes.
- **Correct execution** by updating plays, workflows, and coaching triggers.
- **Prove the correction worked** through micro-experiments, not opinion.

This chapter is about installing those capabilities as a permanent mechanism. Not as a quarterly initiative.

## The Self-Correcting Revenue Loop

A revenue system closes its own gaps when it runs a continuous loop:

1. **Miss capture**: every lost deal, stalled deal, and slipped forecast becomes structured input.
2. **Pattern detection**: the system clusters misses into repeatable failure modes.
3. **Intervention**: updated plays, coaching signals, and workflow constraints deploy into execution.
4. **Verification**: micro-experiments confirm what actually changed outcomes.
5. **Propagation**: what works becomes default behavior, not a slide deck.

If you don't build this loop, you don't have a scaling engine. You have a scaling headcount plan.

## 1) Miss Capture: Stop Treating Loss as Narrative

Most post-loss analysis is theater. A rep selects a loss reason from a dropdown, writes a polite note, and moves on. Leadership reviews "competitive pressures" over coffee. Nothing changes.

Self-correcting execution requires a different design assumption: **loss is data.** And data must be captured as the system operates, not interpreted later.

### Miss capture must include more than "why we lost"

A useful miss record includes:

- **Stage of death**: where the deal stopped progressing.
- **State divergence**: what evidence contradicted the declared stage (stakeholders missing, no mutual plan, procurement introduced late).
- **Time markers**: how long key states persisted (stalled days, response latency windows, approval cycle length).
- **Objection fingerprints**: not "pricing," but which pricing pattern (discount corridor breach, competitor anchor, unbundled value, missing ROI proof).
- **Handoff integrity**: whether internal transitions introduced latency or inconsistency.

This is where organizations quietly under-invest. They keep measuring outcomes and under-measuring failure mechanics. Then they wonder why fixes don't compound.

### What Atlassian understood: capture is multi-channel or it is incomplete

Atlassian's CARE framework—Collect, Analyze, Resolve, Empower—pulls inputs across surveys, support, and social feedback to detect issue patterns and close loops at scale [https://getthematic.com/insights/customer-feedback-loop-examples].

Steal the structure. Lost deals are not just sales events. They are the intersection of product expectations, messaging clarity, onboarding signals, and trust. If miss capture only lives in CRM fields, it will always be politically filtered and structurally late.

## 2) Pattern Detection: Cluster Failures Into Named Failure Modes

"Pricing" is not a pattern. It's an excuse.

A system that closes its own gaps names failure modes precisely enough to correct them. That means clustering misses into repeatable, actionable categories. Not "competitor won." Not "timing."

### The Failure Mode Library (FML): the system's institutional memory

Build a Failure Mode Library: a controlled taxonomy of how deals die in your operating model. Examples:

- **Unmapped buying group**: late-stage motion without economic buyer confirmation.
- **Value proof deficit**: ROI narrative absent before procurement engagement.
- **Procurement surprise**: security/legal introduced after pricing frame set.
- **Latency decay**: response windows widen step-by-step until the deal becomes inert.
- **Over-touch fatigue**: multiple teams contact with conflicting offers and tone.
- **Demo-to-next-step break**: demo occurs, but no mutual action plan is established.

Once you have named failure modes, you stop debating "what happened" and start engineering corrections.

### How monday.com operationalizes pattern detection: find trends, then route action fast

monday.com describes feedback loops that use AI for trend spotting and drive operational response within defined windows (including automated response targets such as within 48 hours), then measure ROI to prioritize fixes [https://monday.com/blog/monday-campaigns/customer-feedback-loop/].

Again, steal the mechanics: pattern detection without response windows and prioritization is just analytics. A self-correcting engine is biased toward action.

## 3) Coaching Signals: Coaching Stops Being a Meeting and Becomes a Trigger

Most coaching is scheduled. That's why it fails.

Skill correction is time-sensitive. If you coach a rep two weeks after a key call, you are not improving performance. You are producing commentary.

A gap-closing system turns coaching into instrumentation: it triggers when patterns appear, and it targets the specific behavior that drove the miss.

### Insight7's call coaching blueprint: build coaching playbooks from actual misses

Insight7 emphasizes using real call recordings to detect patterns in successful and failed behaviors, then build iterative coaching playbooks with continuous review cycles [https://insight7.io/build-coaching-playbooks-from-real-call-examples/].

The structural point is not "record calls." It's this: if execution is partially autonomous, coaching must be partially autonomous too. Not automated pep talks. Triggered, behavior-specific correction tied to observed evidence.

### Coaching signals must route to the right layer

Not every gap is a rep gap. A mature system routes coaching signals by origin:

- **Rep-level**: discovery depth, stakeholder mapping, objection handling.
- **Manager-level**: inspection misses, weak deal qualification discipline, inconsistent forecasts.
- **System-level**: wrong routing, broken handoffs, inconsistent definitions, playbook drift.

If you treat system gaps as rep problems, you will train forever and improve never.

## 4) Playbook Refinement: Playbooks Are Not Documents. They Are Deployed Behavior.

Most playbooks are written like literature. Elegant. Ignored.

A playbook only matters when it is executable: embedded in workflow, triggered by events, constrained by governance, and updated without fanfare.

### RevenueHero: the demo funnel as a closed-loop learning surface

RevenueHero's demo funnel playbook explicitly references post-demo surveys, sales debriefs, and lost-deal analysis to track conversion metrics and iterate messaging and process [https://www.revenuehero.io/blog/the-revops-playbook-for-a-high-converting-demo-funnel].

The demo is a failure factory when it isn't instrumented. Teams celebrate a "great demo," then wonder why the deal dies. RevenueHero's structure matters because it treats the demo as a measurable system transition, not a performance moment.

### SENNEBOGEN: objection handling as packaged system output

In SENNEBOGEN's HubSpot revenue engine case study, the company built sales-to-marketing feedback loops, shared dashboards, and objection-handling packages—supporting alignment and reported revenue impact ($9.3M) with reduced reliance on constant intervention [https://digitalj2.com/2026/02/17/how-a-manufacturing-leader-built-a-direct-revenue-engine-using-hubspot-case-study/].

Ignore the branding. Observe the redesign: objections became an asset the system packages and propagates, not a problem each rep relearns alone. That is gap closure as operating leverage.

### The Playbook Deployment Rule

A playbook change is not "announced." It is:

- **encoded** into orchestration logic,
- **attached** to the moments it is needed,
- **measured** by downstream outcomes,
- **reversible** if it degrades performance.

If your playbooks require belief and memory, you have documentation. Not execution architecture.

## 5) Micro-Experiments: Stop Arguing. Start Isolating Causality.

Most revenue teams "iterate" by consensus. That is slow and usually wrong.

A self-correcting revenue engine runs micro-experiments continuously: small, controlled changes that prove what actually moves the system.

### Micro-experiments have three constraints

- **Controlled scope**: one segment, one stage, one play variant.
- **Single primary metric**: win rate at that stage, time-to-next-step, demo-to-opportunity conversion, discount incidence.
- **Short feedback horizon**: measured in days or weeks, not quarters.

This is how systems learn fast without destabilizing production execution.

### monday.com's ROI tracking requirement is the missing discipline

monday.com frames feedback loops not just as collection and response, but as ROI-tracked prioritization that determines what gets fixed first [https://monday.com/blog/monday-campaigns/customer-feedback-loop/].

Revenue systems need the same posture: experiments aren't "learning." They are capital allocation. You are spending attention and risk budget to buy certainty about what compounds.

## What "Self-Correcting" Looks Like in Practice

Put the loop into an operational sequence. Here's the mature pattern.

### Step 1: Instrument misses automatically

- Lost deal triggers a structured capture workflow.
- Post-demo surveys and debriefs attach to outcome states [https://www.revenuehero.io/blog/the-revops-playbook-for-a-high-converting-demo-funnel].
- Customer feedback from multiple channels is collected continuously, not when someone remembers [https://getthematic.com/insights/customer-feedback-loop-examples].

**Step 2: Convert raw misses into named failure modes**

- Weekly pattern runs that cluster reasons and evidence signals.
- Failure Mode Library updated under governance, not opinion.

**Step 3: Trigger playbook corrections and coaching signals**

- Call pattern emerges → coaching play deployed in workflow [https://insight7.io/build-coaching-playbooks-from-real-call-examples/].
- Objection cluster rises → objection-handling package updated and routed to the field [https://digitalj2.com/2026/02/17/how-a-manufacturing-leader-built-a-direct-revenue-engine-using-hubspot-case-study/].

**Step 4: Run micro-experiments to verify improvement**

- One change, one segment, one metric.
- Roll forward what works. Roll back what doesn't.

### Step 5: Propagate silently

The correction becomes default behavior. No enablement theater required. The system simply executes the new reality.

## The Hidden Failure Modes (And Why Most "Feedback Loops" Don't Close)

### Failure Mode 1: Collection without resolution

Teams love collecting feedback. It feels rigorous. It's also cheap. Resolution is expensive because it forces trade-offs and ownership. Atlassian's CARE framework explicitly includes Resolve and Empower, not just collection and analysis [https://getthematic.com/insights/customer-feedback-loop-examples].

If your loop stops at insight, you built a reporting system. Not a self-correcting engine.

### Failure Mode 2: Coaching that produces compliance, not capability

If coaching is generic and scheduled, it becomes culture signaling. If coaching is evidence-triggered, it becomes capability compounding [https://insight7.io/build-coaching-playbooks-from-real-call-examples/].

### Failure Mode 3: Playbook updates that don't deploy

A playbook that lives in enablement software is a library. A playbook that lives in orchestration logic is an operating system. SENNEBOGEN's case is instructive precisely because it created packages and loops that could be used repeatedly without constant re-translation [https://digitalj2.com/2026/02/17/how-a-manufacturing-leader-built-a-direct-revenue-engine-using-hubspot-case-study/].

### Failure Mode 4: Experiments that are too big to learn from

When experiments are broad, results are ambiguous. Ambiguity creates debate. Debate creates delay. Delay recreates the original problem: humans as the bottleneck.

## The Executive Redesign: Your Job Becomes Loop Integrity

A self-correcting revenue system reduces the need for constant leadership intervention. It does not reduce the need for leadership. It changes where leadership applies force.

In the old model, leaders pushed execution. In the new model, leaders govern the loop:

- **What must be captured?**
- **Which failure modes matter most?**
- **Who owns the correction mechanism?**
- **How are playbooks deployed into workflow?**
- **Which experiments are allowed, and how is risk contained?**

This is how you scale without becoming the system's permanent supervisor.

## The Inevitable Implication: Companies Will Separate by How Fast They Stop Making the Same Mistake

When autonomy enters the revenue stack, everyone gets faster execution. That advantage collapses. Speed becomes table stakes.

Durable advantage shifts to something rarer: how quickly your system identifies failure, corrects it, and prevents repetition.

Most organizations will keep losing deals and holding reviews. A few will lose deals and update the machine.

Those companies will feel unnervingly consistent—not because they are lucky, but because their execution closes its own gaps.

Chapter 13

# Where Humans Create Irreplaceable Value

## The Seller Was Never Paid for Activity. The Seller Was Paid for Judgment.

Agentic revenue systems will absorb the majority of what most organizations historically called "sales work": sequencing, follow-up, routing, summarization, coordination, and basic qualification.

That does not eliminate the human seller. It removes the economic camouflage.

When the system can execute the routine end-to-end, every remaining human hour becomes legible. Boards will stop funding headcount as "coverage." They will fund headcount as *judgment capacity*.

This chapter is the redesign required on the human side of the architecture. Because the most expensive failure in an agentic transition is not adopting agents. It is keeping humans positioned as if agents don't exist.

## The Shift: From Producers of Motion to Owners of Trust

In the pre-agentic era, sales teams were engines of motion. They generated activity because activity was the only scalable mechanism available.

In the agentic era, motion becomes cheap. Trust does not.

So the job changes:

- **Old role design:** humans produce volume, managers inspect volume, systems document volume.
- **New role design:** systems produce volume, humans produce trust, leaders govern where trust is deployed.

This is already visible in human-first sales operating designs that measure relationship depth over raw output and redeploy sellers toward high-effort, high-trust touches rather than quota-chasing theater [https://www.punchb2b.com/blog/your-2026-guide-to-human-first-sales].

## The Four Human Value Roles (And the Work They Replace)

Autonomy does not eliminate jobs. It eliminates *misallocated cognition*. Humans become most valuable when the interaction requires beliefs to change, risk to be carried, or trade-offs to be negotiated.

In an agentic revenue system, humans converge into four roles. Not job titles. Economic functions.

### 1) Trust Builder: The Human as Risk Absorber

Trust building is not "relationship skills." It is the act of reducing perceived risk inside a buying committee that cannot afford to be wrong.

Trust is measurable demand in the market, not a soft preference. Some buyer research summaries put the priority bluntly: a large share of buyers rank trust as a leading factor, and meaningful trust often requires multiple interactions rather than a single persuasive moment [https://owenvansyckle.com/the-role-of-trust-in-the-buyer-seller-relationship/].

Agents can inform. Agents can respond. Agents can keep cadence. But they cannot credibly *carry* risk when the buyer needs someone accountable on the other side of the table.

Where trust builders outperform automation:

- **Moments of perceived downside:** security review, procurement escalation, executive scrutiny.
- **Moments of emotional volatility:** a failure, an outage, a stakeholder conflict, a political reversal.

- **Moments of accountability:** "If this goes wrong, who owns it?"

This is why "human touch" frameworks keep mapping crisis management to humans: empathy, negotiation, and irreducible accountability are not automatable without damaging trust precisely when trust is most valuable [https://www.dinamikcrm.com/en/blog/the-power-of-human-touch].

### 2) Storyteller: The Human as Meaning-Maker

Most revenue orgs still treat messaging as a marketing artifact. In practice, the deal is won by narrative coherence: why change, why now, why you, and why the buyer won't regret it later.

Agents can generate copy. They cannot create *earned relevance* without human witness—someone who listened, understood, and returned with a story that the buyer recognizes as true.

One of the more instructive modern cases is not "AI content." It's what happened when humans did the hard interpretive work: buyer interviews surfaced real worker constraints, which became a narrative the market trusted—turning operations reality (the "scan-off" challenge) into differentiated story and sales effectiveness [https://flashworksmarketing.com/b2b-marketing-story-trust/].

That's what storytelling does in an agentic world:

- It translates complexity into conviction.
- It turns features into stakes.
- It creates internal alignment inside the buyer's organization.

Automation scales language. Humans scale meaning. Meaning is what moves committees.

### 3) Strategic Guide: The Human as Navigation Layer

When execution becomes autonomous, buyers don't need more follow-up. They need better decisions.

The strategic guide is not a "solutions consultant." This role owns navigation: diagnosing constraints, sequencing decisions, and preventing the buyer from making the wrong trade-off for the wrong reason.

Human-first sales designs already emphasize shifting sellers toward advisory work across the buyer journey—retention, expansion, and high-quality interaction—while the system carries the routine [https://www.punchb2b.com/blog/your-2026-guide-to-human-first-sales].

The DinamikCRM framing is unusually practical here: humans dominate where strategic advisory requires context shaping, negotiation of priorities, and custom solution design—while routine execution is delegated to AI and workflows [https://www.dinamikcrm.com/en/blog/the-power-of-human-touch].

Where strategic guides outperform automation:

- **Multi-constraint design:** budget, security, timeline, internal adoption, political risk.
- **Ambiguity resolution:** "What is the real problem we're solving?"
- **Change choreography:** helping the buyer win internally, not just select a vendor.

This is also why the next sales org shape looks different: fewer humans supervising more autonomous capacity, with human effort concentrated around expertise, guidance, and implementation support rather than mechanical coverage [https://www.saastr.com/the-2026-sales-reckoning-why-your-traditional-sales-team-is-about-to-look-very-different/].

### 4) Deal Strategist: The Human as Non-Linear Negotiator

Many deals stall not because the buyer is unconvinced, but because the deal becomes non-linear: risk allocation, legal posture, procurement tactics, internal politics, and competitive framing collide.

Agents can propose options. They cannot read the room, detect the hidden veto, or reframe the negotiation without escalating conflict.

Deal strategists create value where the "next best action" is not a best action at all—because the buyer is not optimizing for speed, but for safety and internal legitimacy.

Where deal strategists outperform automation:

- **Procurement dynamics:** trading terms, not just price.
- **Competitive displacement:** reframing switching risk and incumbent advantage.
- **Internal sponsor defense:** equipping a champion to survive scrutiny.
- **High-stakes exceptions:** anything irreversible, precedent-setting, or margin-defining.

## The Human/Agent Boundary: The Interactions That Must Stay Human

The mistake leaders make is drawing the boundary by channel: "emails can be automated, calls stay human." That is amateur thinking.

The boundary is set by four conditions:

- **Irreversibility:** once sent/committed, it cannot be cleanly undone.
- **Ambiguity:** the right move depends on context the system cannot reliably formalize.
- **Asymmetry:** one side is carrying materially more risk than the other.
- **Identity exposure:** the interaction affects credibility, trust, and perceived intent.

This maps cleanly to the "human touch" partitioning that keeps crisis management and strategic advisory human-led, while delegating routine work to AI [https://www.dinamikcrm.com/en/blog/the-power-of-human-touch].

If you're redesigning roles honestly, your question becomes:

**Where do we have non-linear outcomes?**

That is where humans belong.

## Role Redesign: The Sales Org Stops Being a Ladder and Becomes a Control System

The traditional sales org was built as a ladder: SDR → AE → Enterprise AE → Management. It implied that career growth meant owning more accounts and more motion.

Agentic revenue breaks that logic. Because "more motion" is no longer a human achievement. It is system throughput.

So the org becomes a control system: humans are placed where they increase trust density, reduce risk, and close complex trade-offs. Everything else is execution fabric.

### The Supervision Ratio: 2–3 Humans Overseeing Agentic Capacity

A practical pattern emerging in forward-looking revenue org design is the supervision ratio: a few humans overseeing multiple autonomous agents, with humans anchoring deep expertise, strategic guidance, and implementation support [https://www.saastr.com/the-2026-sales-reckoning-why-your-traditional-sales-team-is-about-to-look-very-different/].

This is not headcount reduction as a hobby. It is the reallocation of labor to where labor changes outcomes.

### Territory Design Becomes Buyer-Journey Design

When systems handle coverage, territories stop being lists of accounts and become maps of *buyer states.*

Human-first role models already shift focus toward the buyer journey and relationship depth rather than quota-driven volume, using AI to amplify high-effort human touches (video, direct mail, high-context outreach) instead of replacing them [https://www.punchb2b.com/blog/your-2026-guide-to-human-first-sales].

A modern territory is not "N accounts." It is "N high-trust moments."

## Comp Redesign: Pay Humans for What Agents Cannot Do

Comp plans are operating instructions. Most comp plans still instruct humans to do what the system should do: maximize activity, chase early-stage coverage, and manufacture pipeline.

That becomes structurally wrong once your system can create and manage motion continuously.

In an agentic revenue system, comp needs to price the four human roles explicitly.

### Principle 1: Measure Relationship Depth, Not Activity Volume

If trust is the product, depth has to be measured and rewarded. Human-first sales guidance increasingly emphasizes relationship depth as the metric that matters, using AI to remove low-value busywork and amplify high-effort human touches [https://www.punchb2b.com/blog/your-2026-guide-to-human-first-sales].

If you keep paying for raw activity, you will get automation-driven noise with human signatures attached.

### Principle 2: Pay for De-Risking, Not Just Closing

Closing is an outcome. De-risking is the mechanism that makes outcomes repeatable.

This is where trust-builder behavior becomes economically legible: fewer late-stage reversals, fewer procurement surprises, fewer "we went dark" failures. Trust is not a feeling. Trust is reduced volatility.

### Principle 3: Pay for Narrative Conversion

If human storytelling is what turns complexity into conviction, then it must show up in how you value work: higher multi-threading, faster stakeholder alignment, improved stage-to-stage conversion in the moments where narrative is the binding constraint.

The Flashworks story illustrates the mechanism: real buyer interviews produced a worker-centered narrative that built trust and differentiation in market conversations—something automation cannot originate without human truth-gathering [https://flashworksmarketing.com/b2b-marketing-story-trust/].

### Principle 4: Pay for Deal Integrity in Complex Cycles

Negotiate the right outcome, not just the fast one. Pay for protecting margin corridors, for reducing term and scope ambiguity, and for preserving long-term account viability. Deal strategists should be rewarded for fewer bad wins, not more rushed wins.

## The Failure Mode: "Humans as Approvers" and Other Expensive Misuse

When autonomy rises, the lazy redesign is to make humans the approval layer: everything the agent does waits for a rep or manager to sign off.

That is not role redesign. That is bureaucracy disguised as safety.

Humans are not valuable because they can click "approve." Humans are valuable because they can:

- absorb risk,
- hold accountability,
- change beliefs,
- and negotiate non-linear trade-offs.

If your humans are spending time approving routine motion, your architecture is telling you something: either your guardrails are immature, or your leaders are using people to compensate for missing governance.

## What This Means Operationally: A Human Time Budget

You cannot redesign roles without budgeting human attention. In an agentic system, attention becomes the scarcest asset because execution is no longer scarce.

A functional operating policy is simple:

- **Agents handle:** volume, routing, sequencing, persistence, documentation, and continuous follow-through.
- **Humans handle:** trust, narrative, high-stakes guidance, and complex deal strategy.

The trust research summaries make the point mechanically: trust is prioritized by buyers and typically requires repeated, high-quality interactions to form—especially in multi-stakeholder environments [https://owenvansyckle.com/the-role-of-trust-in-the-buyer-seller-relationship/]. Those interactions must be reserved for humans, then protected from being consumed by the coordination work the system can do.

## The Inevitable Implication: The Best Sales Teams Will Look Smaller—and Be More Expensive

The highest-performing agentic revenue organizations will employ fewer humans in the middle. Not because they value humans less. Because they refuse to waste them.

They will concentrate human roles where human judgment changes outcomes, then use the system to provide:

- continuous detection,
- continuous orchestration,
- and continuous follow-through.

The result is counterintuitive but predictable: human teams become smaller, calmer, and more senior. They do less motion. They carry more trust. They do not "run the pipeline." They govern the relationships and decisions that the pipeline depends on.

Competitors who keep humans positioned as activity engines will look busy. They will also look increasingly average. Because in an agentic world, motion is not a differentiator. Judgment is.

Chapter 14

# Data Quality, Governance, and Signal Integrity

## The Most Dangerous Lie in Modern Revenue: "Our Data Is Good Enough."

In the dashboard era, "good enough" data was survivable. Humans translated. Humans reconciled. Humans applied judgment to messy truth.

In the agentic era, "good enough" becomes a liability. Because the system doesn't just *analyze* your data. It *acts* on it.

That is the quiet trade most leadership teams have not internalized:

- **Bad data in a reporting system** produces arguments.
- **Bad data in an execution system** produces customer impact.

This chapter is not a plea for better hygiene. It is a structural warning. Autonomous revenue systems are only as trustworthy as the signals they consume—and the governance that constrains what they are allowed to do with them.

## The Shift: Data as Documentation → Data as Authority

Most companies still govern revenue data as if it were a record-keeping artifact. Fields get cleaned for forecasting calls. Duplicates get addressed when they cause embarrassment. Access gets discussed when security asks.

Agentic systems force a different frame: data is no longer a description of the business. Data becomes delegated authority.

If an autonomous system can route an account, trigger outreach, change status, prioritize an opportunity, or generate a customer-facing message, then your data models are not "information models." They are *control surfaces.*

That is why data quality, governance, and signal integrity are not RevOps concerns. They are board-level operating concerns.

## Signal Integrity: The Metric Boards Will Eventually Demand

Executives love metrics that are too late to be useful. Pipeline accuracy at quarter close. Churn after renewal has gone sideways. Win rate after the market has moved.

Signal integrity is different. Signal integrity is an upstream measure of whether the autonomous system is perceiving reality accurately enough to act safely.

This is not a metaphor borrowed from engineering for style. In autonomous vehicle control hardware, signal integrity is treated as a decisive constraint because high-speed systems fail when signals degrade—hence disciplined design and testing methods to prevent corrupted interpretation downstream [https://www.allpcb.com/blog/pcb-knowledge/signal-integrity-challenges-in-autonomous-vehicle-control-pcb-design.html].

Revenue autonomy has the same constraint. Different substrate. Same physics: when signals degrade, the system makes confident moves for the wrong reasons—at speed.

### Define signal integrity (for revenue)

**Signal integrity is the probability that a revenue-relevant event, attribute, or state change is:**

- **Accurate** (it reflects reality)
- **Timely** (it arrives before decisions are made)
- **Complete** (critical context is present)
- **Consistent** (it means the same thing across systems)
- **Traceable** (you can explain lineage and transformation)
- **Permissioned** (access and use are constrained by policy)

If you cannot defend those properties, you are not running an autonomous revenue system. You are running an automation engine on disputed reality.

## The Unsexy Work: Hygiene, Enrichment, Taxonomy, Access Control

Most "data initiatives" fail because they are framed as cleanliness projects. They become indefinite. Political. Under-owned.

Treat them instead as four execution prerequisites. Not to "improve analytics." To make autonomy governable.

### 1) Hygiene: Make the system resistant to rot

Hygiene is not a one-time cleanup. It is continuous monitoring and correction of quality drift. If data quality is not continuously measured, you will slowly rebuild the same chaos you just paid to remove.

Pragmatic governance guidance recommends automated quality checks and continuous monitoring precisely because manual audits cannot keep up with operational velocity [https://www.anomalo.com/blog/5-data-governance-best-practices/]. Coherent Solutions pushes the same direction: continuous data quality monitoring and automated workflows for routine hygiene tasks so the system doesn't depend on quarterly heroics [https://www.coherentsolutions.com/insights/ai-powered-data-governance-implementing-best-practices-and-frameworks].

### Hygiene is the minimum viable truth for action

In agentic revenue, hygiene is not "nice to have." It is the boundary between safe execution and reputational damage. The only hygiene that matters is execution-grade hygiene:

- **Identity integrity**: one account is one account (dedupe, match, merge)
- **State integrity**: stages and statuses cannot be cosmetically advanced
- **Contact integrity**: opt-outs, roles, and stakeholder changes are current
- **Time integrity**: timestamps reflect actual sequence of events

If you cannot trust identity and state, you cannot trust orchestration. And if you cannot trust orchestration, autonomy becomes a brand risk multiplier.

### 2) Enrichment: Fill context gaps without manufacturing fiction

Enrichment is where many teams accidentally corrupt their own system. They treat third-party append as "truth." They overwrite verified internal reality with probabilistic external guesses. Then they wonder why routing, segmentation, and personalization degrade.

A mature approach treats enrichment as *probabilistic* until verified. It is additive, not authoritative—unless you can trace lineage and confidence. Coherent Solutions highlights lineage and tracking as part of modern governance because the system needs to know where facts came from and how they were derived [https://www.coherentsolutions.com/insights/ai-powered-data-governance-implementing-best-practices-and-frameworks].

### Enrichment rules that preserve integrity

- **Never overwrite first-party truth automatically.** Append, compare, then promote with rules.
- **Enforce source ranking.** Some sources can inform; fewer sources can decide.
- **Capture confidence and provenance.** "We think this is the CFO" is not the same as "this is the CFO."
- **Instrument enrichment fallout.** Track how often enrichment causes downstream exceptions (misroutes, bounces, opt-out violations).

Enrichment is valuable when it closes coverage gaps. It is destructive when it creates false precision.

### 3) Taxonomy: Stop debating what words mean

Taxonomy sounds academic until you try to run autonomous actions across teams. Then it becomes the difference between coordination and internal collision.

If marketing's "engaged" contradicts sales' "qualified," the system can do only two things:

- act inconsistently, or
- escalate constantly.

Either way, you lose autonomy.

Governance best-practice frameworks repeatedly include standardized definitions and structured approaches because without semantic alignment, quality checks and controls are cosmetic [https://hatchworks.com/blog/data-governance/best-practices-for-data-governance/]. Dataversity's guidance on adapting governance for autonomous and generative AI stresses harmonization and reliability—because autonomous systems amplify semantic mismatch into operational error [https://www.dataversity.net/articles/adapting-data-governance-for-autonomous-and-generative-ai/].

### The practical revenue taxonomy that matters

You do not need a universal ontology. You need a small set of enforced, cross-functional truth objects and states:

- **Account state**: target → active → in-cycle → customer → renewal window

- **Opportunity state**: stage progression tied to evidence, not optimism
- **Buying group roles**: economic buyer, champion, technical evaluator, risk owner
- **Risk states**: stalled momentum, stakeholder instability, procurement activation, margin risk
- **Suppression states**: do-not-contact conditions, active legal/procurement, fatigue thresholds

Taxonomy is what turns "we should align" into "the system cannot contradict us."

### 4) Access control: Autonomy makes data exposure operational, not theoretical

When autonomous systems operate, data is no longer accessed only by humans inside well-understood roles. Agents request. Agents retrieve. Agents transform. Agents act.

That means access control is no longer about internal privacy hygiene. It becomes your protection against two failures that destroy trust fast:

- **Unauthorized disclosure** (sensitive customer details used in the wrong context)

- **Unauthorized action** (sensitive data driving decisions it should not be allowed to influence)

Governance guidance continues to emphasize security measures—encryption, authentication, access restrictions—because trustworthy decision systems require controlled exposure, especially around sensitive information [https://www.anomalo.com/blog/5-data-governance-best-practices/]. Coherent Solutions makes access control central in AI-driven governance practices for sensitive data environments [https://www.coherentsolutions.com/insights/ai-powered-data-governance-implementing-best-practices-and-frameworks]. Dataversity frames the governance adaptation explicitly for autonomous and generative contexts, with a stronger need for platform-based security and privacy controls as autonomy rises [https://www.dataversity.net/articles/adapting-data-governance-for-autonomous-and-generative-ai/].

### The access-control redesign revenue leaders must make

- **From role-based to action-based controls.** Not "who can see," but "what can be done with what."

- **From static permissions to context permissions.** Segment, region, policy state, and customer status should constrain access and action.
- **From audit logs to auditability by design.** Traceability must be usable, not forensic art.

Access control is no longer the security team's perimeter. It is the operating system's steering lock.

## Governance Must Evolve: From Policy Documents to Executable Constraints

Most governance is written for humans. It assumes discretion. It assumes interpretation. It assumes enforcement is a training problem.

Agents don't interpret policy. They either have constraints, or they don't.

Dataversity's guidance on governance for autonomous and generative AI is direct about the need to adapt governance frameworks and enforce reliability practices—because ungoverned autonomy amplifies error and exposure [https://www.dataversity.net/articles/adapting-data-governance-for-autonomous-and-generative-ai/]. Hatchworks frames governance as a structured program with audits and role clarity, not an ad hoc afterthought [https://hatchworks.com/blog/data-governance/best-practices-for-data-governance/].

### The modern governance stack (for agentic revenue)

- **Standards**: declared definitions, required fields, allowed ranges, allowed claims
- **Controls**: automated checks, anomaly detection, continuous monitoring
- **Permissions**: what data and actions are allowed by segment and risk class
- **Lineage**: traceable transformations and sources of truth
- **Audit and rollback**: observable actions with the ability to reverse

This is the shift: governance becomes part of execution, not an external review of execution.

## The "Signal Integrity Board Pack": What You Report When Autonomy Is Real

Boards do not need another dashboard. They need confidence that the revenue machine is perceiving reality cleanly enough to act without creating damage.

Signal integrity becomes reportable when you treat it like an operating metric, not a vague aspiration.

### Signal integrity KPIs that actually matter

- **Truth divergence rate**: % of key metrics that differ across "official" systems
- **Critical-field completeness**: for fields that trigger action (not fields that make CRM look tidy)
- **Freshness/SLA adherence**: time-to-availability for events that drive orchestration
- **Identity collision rate**: duplicate accounts/contacts that produce conflicting actions
- **Exception rate caused by data**: escalations triggered by missing/contradictory inputs
- **Access violations prevented**: blocked attempts by agents/workflows to retrieve or use restricted data
- **Lineage coverage**: % of decision-driving attributes with traceable provenance

Anomalo's framing of governance best practices includes the operational basics—standards, automated checks, security measures—that make these metrics measurable instead of performative [https://www.anomalo.com/blog/5-data-governance-best-practices/]. Coherent Solutions similarly emphasizes continuous monitoring and lineage support as part of making governance real at runtime, not theoretical at audit time [https://www.coherentsolutions.com/insights/ai-powered-data-governance-implementing-best-practices-and-frameworks].

## The Failure Modes That Kill Autonomy (Quietly)

Most autonomy programs don't fail because the system can't generate outputs. They fail because the organization cannot trust the outputs enough to let them execute. That trust hinges on signal integrity.

### Failure Mode 1: "Automation-grade data" pretending to be "execution-grade data"

Automation-grade data is a partial truth that can create tasks. Execution-grade data is a governed truth that can trigger customer impact. When companies confuse the two, they get early "wins" and late incidents.

### Failure Mode 2: Taxonomy drift creates internal conflict at machine speed

If every function retains its private definitions, orchestration becomes multiplication of contradictions. The system doesn't unify the company. It accelerates its fragmentation. Governance frameworks exist to prevent exactly this outcome: standards first, then automation, then scale [https://hatchworks.com/blog/data-governance/best-practices-for-data-governance/].

### Failure Mode 3: Agents become a new class of privileged user

When agents can "see everything" to be helpful, they inevitably do something with sensitive data that creates exposure. This is why governance must evolve specifically for autonomous and generative systems—because the access pattern changes from occasional human queries to continuous machine retrieval and use [https://www.dataversity.net/articles/adapting-data-governance-for-autonomous-and-generative-ai/].

### Failure Mode 4: No lineage, no accountability

If you cannot explain why the system believed something, you cannot govern outcomes. You can only react to incidents. Lineage is not documentation. It is how you keep autonomy accountable when it moves faster than meetings. Continuous lineage and monitoring are positioned as core mechanisms in modern AI-driven governance approaches for this reason [https://www.coherentsolutions.com/insights/ai-powered-data-governance-implementing-best-practices-and-frameworks].

## The Executive Redesign: From "Data Cleanup" to "Signal Integrity Program"

Most leaders delegate data to ops and security, then wonder why autonomy stalls. Signal integrity is not a back-office quality initiative. It is a revenue control initiative.

### The pragmatic program (what actually works)

- **Declare the minimum viable truth for action.** Not every field. The ones that drive autonomous decisions.
- **Install continuous monitoring.** Quality checks that run at the cadence of execution, not the cadence of audits [https://www.anomalo.com/blog/5-data-governance-best-practices/]

[https://www.coherentsolutions.com/insights/ai-powered-data-governance-implementing-best-practices-and-frameworks].

- **Enforce a shared taxonomy for states that trigger action.** Harmonize definitions that orchestrate cross-functional motion [https://www.dataversity.net/articles/adapting-data-governance-for-autonomous-and-generative-ai/].
- **Permission by action class.** Constrain what agents can do with customer data, and under what contexts [https://www.coherentsolutions.com/insights/ai-powered-data-governance-implementing-best-practices-and-frameworks].
- **Establish auditability and regular review.** Not as compliance theater, but as operational governance that keeps autonomy safe as it scales [https://hatchworks.com/blog/data-governance/best-practices-for-data-governance/].

This is how you stop treating data as a cleanup task and start treating it as the integrity layer of execution.

## The Inevitable Implication: Signal Integrity Becomes Competitive Advantage

As autonomous execution spreads, the market won't separate companies by who has agents. It will separate them by whose agents can be trusted to act.

Trust will not be won through vendor claims. It will be won through signal integrity:

- clean enough to execute,
- governed enough to be safe,
- traceable enough to be accountable,
- and disciplined enough to improve without incidents.

The companies that treat data as authority—and govern it accordingly—will scale autonomy calmly. Everyone else will keep "piloting agents" and quietly increasing risk.

Chapter 15

# Managing Brand, Compliance, and Reputation Risk

## The Fastest Way to Lose Trust Is to Scale Speech Without Control

Revenue leaders are building systems that can speak and act at machine cadence. Legal, compliance, and brand leaders are not "anti-innovation" for resisting it. They are responding to a structural reality:

**When outbound execution becomes autonomous, reputation becomes an engineering problem.**

In the pre-agentic era, risk was bounded by headcount. A bad email was one person's mistake. In the agentic era, a bad message is a system behavior. It repeats. It propagates. It becomes discoverable.

This is why brand and compliance concerns feel existential in autonomous revenue. They are. Because autonomy doesn't just increase output. It increases *blast radius*.

## The Shift: From "Guidelines" to Constraints

Most organizations attempt to govern outbound behavior with documents: brand voice guidelines, messaging playbooks, legal disclaimers, approved claims lists.

That governance model assumes two things:

- Humans will remember, interpret, and comply.
- Violations will be rare enough to correct socially.

Autonomous agents invalidate both. They don't "remember." They don't "interpret." They execute.

So the operating model must change:

**Brand and compliance move from training to enforcement.**

The practical mechanism is simple and non-negotiable: if you want autonomous execution, you must convert intent into enforceable constraints. That means policies-as-code.

## The Non-Obvious Lesson From Reputation Collapse: Oversight Fails Quietly Until It Doesn't

Reputation failures rarely begin as dramatic scandals. They begin as governance blind spots.

The Cambridge Analytica episode is remembered as a privacy controversy. The more operational truth is that a trust system ran without sufficient monitoring and constraint—and the cost showed up as market value loss and global scrutiny [https://riskandinsurance.com/4-reputation-case-studies/].

The same pattern repeats in other cases: cultural and operational risks that leadership treated as local issues became enterprise liabilities with litigation and reputational consequences [https://riskandinsurance.com/4-reputation-case-studies/].

Autonomous agents amplify this exact failure mode because they create two accelerants:

- **They externalize internal contradictions.** If your teams disagree, the agent can express that disagreement to customers.
- **They operationalize weak oversight.** If you can't see what's happening, the system will still act.

Legal leaders are not worried about AI. They are worried about *unmonitored outbound behavior*. That is a rational concern, with precedent.

## The Brand/Compliance Control Stack (What Must Exist Before You Scale Autonomy)

If you want to move fast without gambling your reputation, you need a control stack with five layers:

1. **Language constraints** (what the system is allowed to say)
2. **Policies-as-code** (what the system is allowed to do)
3. **Outbound activity monitoring** (what the system actually did)
4. **Auditability** (why it did it, and who owns it)
5. **Rapid rollback** (how you stop and reverse damage)

This is not "risk management." This is the cost of scaling execution authority.

## 1) Constrain Language Like a Product Surface, Not a Brand Guideline

The most common executive mistake is treating agent language as "marketing copy." It is not. It is customer-facing behavior.

Your constraints must be enforceable at runtime:

- **Claims constraints:** what outcomes can be stated, with which qualifiers.
- **Regulated language constraints:** forbidden terms, required disclosures, jurisdiction rules.

- **Competitor constraints:** what can be said about others, and what must never be implied.
- **Commitment constraints:** what the system cannot promise (delivery dates, SLAs, legal positions).

The purpose is not to sanitize. It is to preserve intent: you want the system to move fast *inside* your truth boundaries.

If you cannot express "what cannot be said" as a constraint, you do not have governance. You have hope.

## 2) Policies-as-Code: The Only Scalable Form of Compliance

Policies-as-code is not a security trend. It is the missing execution primitive for governed autonomy.

Policy-as-code formalizes rules so systems can enforce them automatically—least privilege access, approved configurations, and standardized controls—rather than relying on manual checks and exceptions [https://www.strongdm.com/what-is/policy-as-code].

Revenue leaders should translate that directly:

- What data can the agent access, by segment and context?
- What channels can it use, and when?
- What action classes are permitted without review?
- What actions require escalation because they are irreversible or precedent-setting?

Policies-as-code turns brand and compliance from "review after the fact" into "prevent the violation." That is the only model that scales.

### 3) Outbound Monitoring: Trust Requires Observability

In autonomous systems, outbound activity is no longer a byproduct. It is a production surface.

You must be able to answer, without a war room:

- How many customer-facing messages were sent in the last hour?
- Which segments received what claims?
- Which accounts were contacted by multiple functions?

- Where did the system attempt an action and get blocked by policy?
- What changed in behavior after a policy update?

This is not "analytics." It is operational oversight. The same reputational case lessons show why: the cost of weak monitoring shows up when stakeholders realize damage was preventable [https://riskandinsurance.com/4-reputation-case-studies/].

## 4) Auditability: If You Can't Explain It, You Can't Defend It

Auditability is not a compliance checkbox. It is your defense mechanism when something goes wrong.

A mature audit trail includes:

- **What** was sent or executed
- **When** it happened
- **To whom** it happened
- **Which policy** allowed it
- **Which inputs** influenced it

- **Which version** of the prompt/policy/play was active

This is where most organizations lose credibility during incidents: they cannot clearly say what happened, so they cannot credibly say it won't happen again.

The reputational recoveries that actually work share a trait: they create clarity fast and communicate it cleanly. Johnson & Johnson's Tylenol response is the classic example—decisive action and transparency restored trust rather than prolonging ambiguity [https://bryghtpath.com/reputation-management-case-studies/].

Auditability is how you enable that posture in an agentic environment. You can't be transparent if you can't see.

## 5) Rapid Rollback: The Capability That Separates "Fast" From "Reckless"

Most executives talk about "moving fast." Few have built the only mechanism that makes speed safe:

**The ability to stop, reverse, and contain.**

In modern engineering organizations, policy-as-code is used with phased enforcement: warn-first modes, gradual rollout, versioning, and controlled escalation to prevent disruptions while still tightening governance [https://www.harness.io/blog/best-practices-for-using-policy-as-code-in-ci-cd-pipelines-with-harness].

Steal that operating discipline for revenue autonomy:

- **Phased enforcement**: policies run in "observe" mode before they run in "block" mode.
- **Versioned policies**: every constraint change is traceable, reviewable, and reversible.
- **Segmented rollout**: expand autonomy by lane, not by enthusiasm.
- **Kill switches**: immediate stop of outbound behavior by channel, segment, or play.
- **Rollback drills**: practiced, not imagined.

A rollback is not a technical detail. It is a governance promise: "We can take risk without making it permanent."

## The Safe Experimentation Pattern: Run Autonomy Like a Controlled Release, Not a Company-Wide Personality

Most "AI risk" stories are not about intelligence. They are about uncontrolled rollout.

A safe experimentation design has four properties:

- **Bounded lanes**: small, explicit scope of allowed action.
- **Observable behavior**: monitoring designed before scale.
- **Auditable change**: policy and prompt versions tracked like production code.
- **Rollback authority**: someone can stop it immediately without debate.

This is how you earn autonomy, instead of announcing it.

## The Crisis Casebook: What Reputation Recovery Actually Looks Like

Autonomous systems don't eliminate crises. They change what a competent response requires. The best corporate recoveries show the same structural moves—moves that map cleanly to agent governance.

### Johnson & Johnson (Tylenol): Decisive Containment + Transparency

The Tylenol recall is remembered as values. It was also operational excellence: contain the damage fast, act visibly, restore confidence through clear steps and communication [https://bryghtpath.com/reputation-management-case-studies/].

Revenue translation:

- When an agent causes an incident, you need immediate containment (kill switch).
- You need a verified explanation (audit trail).
- You need policy updates that prevent repetition (policies-as-code).

You do not "message your way out." You operationally prove control.

### Starbucks: Stop the System, Reset the Rules

Starbucks' response pattern—closing stores for training and changing policies—was not about optics. It was about interrupting execution and resetting operating constraints to prevent repetition [https://bryghtpath.com/reputation-management-case-studies/].

Revenue translation:

- Temporary suspension of autonomous outbound in affected segments.
- Mandatory constraint updates before reactivation.
- Clear communication that the system changed, not just the apology.

### Chipotle: Structural Overhaul After Trust Failure

Chipotle's food safety crisis response is instructive because it required systemic changes—new procedures, monitoring, and operational redesign—not just public statements [https://fastercapital.com/content/Brand-crisis-and-reputation-management--Case-Studies-in-Brand-Crisis-and-Reputation-Management--Lessons-Learned.html].

Revenue translation: when an agent creates customer harm, the fix is rarely "tune the prompt." It is redesign the control surfaces: constraints, monitoring, escalation, rollback.

### Volkswagen: Reputation Damage That Can't Be "Automated Away"

Volkswagen's recovery narrative emphasized stakeholder engagement and rebuilding credibility over time [https://fastercapital.com/content/Brand-crisis-and-reputation-management--Case-Studies-in-Brand-Crisis-and-Reputation-Management--Lessons-Learned.html].

Revenue translation: some actions create long-lived consequences. That's why irreversibility must remain human-governed. Agents can accelerate execution. They cannot carry moral accountability when the market decides intent was wrong.

### Proactive Listening (KFC example clusters): Early Detection Beats Late Apology

Crisis case lessons regularly reinforce proactive monitoring—detecting signals early, responding quickly, and updating operational practices before backlash compounds [https://fastercapital.com/content/Brand-crisis-and-reputation-management--Case-Studies-in-Brand-Crisis-and-reputation-management--Lessons-Learned.html].

Revenue translation: outbound monitoring is not only internal logs. It includes external reaction signals that tell you the system is drifting—fatigue, backlash, confusion, complaint patterns.

## The Executive Contract With Legal, Compliance, and Brand

If you want internal alignment, stop asking for "approval to use agents." That frames autonomy as a tool choice.

Instead, offer a contract:

- **We will constrain language as enforceable rules.**
- **We will implement policies-as-code for permissions and prohibited actions.** [https://www.strongdm.com/what-is/policy-as-code]
- **We will monitor outbound activity continuously.**
- **We will make actions auditable by default.**
- **We will build rollback as an operational capability, not an emergency improvisation.** [https://www.harness.io/blog/best-practices-for-

using-policy-as-code-in-ci-cd-pipelines-with-harness]

That is what serious governance looks like. And it changes the relationship from "blockers vs builders" to joint ownership of a controlled execution system.

## The Inevitable Implication: Reputation Becomes a Systems KPI

In the agentic era, brand is no longer primarily a marketing asset. It becomes a reliability outcome.

Companies that treat outbound autonomy like a controlled release—constrainted, monitored, auditable, reversible—will move faster with less drama. They will look calm because they can contain their own velocity.

Companies that treat autonomy as "scale outreach" will eventually relearn an old lesson at new speed: trust is easy to lose, slow to regain, and brutally expensive once regulators, customers, and the market decide you were careless [https://riskandinsurance.com/4-reputation-case-studies/].

Autonomy will not be judged by how impressive it looks. It will be judged by whether it can be trusted to operate without embarrassing the company. That is not a brand opinion. That is the new operating requirement.

# Part III

# The Migration – Leadership, Economics, and Institutionalization

Chapter 16

# Overcoming Rep Resistance and Change Fatigue

## The Problem Isn't "Adoption." It's Authority.

Sales reps don't resist tools. They resist changes in what the organization is asking them to *be*.

When leaders say, "Our reps are resisting AI," what they usually mean is simpler and more structural:

- The system is trying to take authority without earning trust.
- The new workflow is adding friction without removing workload.
- The organization is changing incentives without changing identity.

This isn't an enablement issue. It's an operating model transition showing up where it always shows up first: in the field, under quota pressure.

## Three Drivers of Resistance (And Why They Are Rational)

### 1) Identity Threat: "You're Replacing the Work That Proved I'm Good."

High-performing reps built their status on skills that were scarce in the old model: persistence, memory, deal orchestration, and personal pipelines of judgment. When the system starts doing that work, the rep doesn't hear "help." They hear "devaluation."

This fear isn't a vibe. It is explicitly documented as a core adoption barrier—job loss anxiety, loss of control, and learning curve fatigue show up consistently in sales AI rollouts [https://smartdev.com/ai-use-cases-in-sales/] [https://www.arionresearch.com/blog/6dp61m5njr1rphynbldc1ov2p5a2n8].

If you ignore identity threat, you get performative compliance:

- They "use" the system the way they "use" the CRM: minimum viable input, maximum private workarounds.
- They protect the parts of their craft the system can't see by refusing to feed it truth.
- They become quietly adversarial—while still hitting number, which makes leadership slow to notice.

### 2) Distrust in Data: "Don't Ask Me to Bet My Quarter on That."

Reps live in a world where false positives cost deals and false negatives cost commissions. They do not have the luxury of experimenting with unreliable signals.

When AI outputs are built on disputed CRM data, broken attribution, incomplete contact graphs, or inconsistent stage definitions, distrust becomes inevitable. This pattern is reinforced in adoption guidance: resistance grows when teams don't understand how outputs are produced, or when poor data leads to visible errors [https://www.arionresearch.com/blog/6dp61m5njr1rphynbldc1ov2p5a2n8] [https://fluint.io/post/ai-sales-agents-101-what-they-are-why-you-need-one].

Executives misread this as "skepticism." It isn't. It's risk management. Reps don't oppose intelligence. They oppose being held accountable to signals they can't validate.

### 3) Tool Overload: "It's Another Tab. Another Score. Another Job."

Sales teams are already carrying a tax: too many systems, too many alerts, too many "insights" that don't close deals. So when leaders introduce "the AI layer," reps don't see leverage. They see more surfaces to maintain.

The adoption literature calls this out directly: prior tech stacks often add noise instead of subtracting workload; AI becomes one more demand unless it collapses work rather than multiplying it [https://smartdev.com/ai-use-cases-in-sales/] [https://fluint.io/post/ai-sales-agents-101-what-they-are-why-you-need-one].

Tool overload produces a predictable behavioral outcome: reps revert to the only system that always works—email, calendar, and their own judgment—then they backfill the "required" tools later, cosmetically.

## The Shift: From Rolling Out Tools to Enrolling Co-Architects

You cannot "deploy" an agentic revenue operating model into a sales organization. You have to *co-design* it with the people who will live inside it.

Not because feelings matter more than results. Because reps are your largest distribution surface for execution truth. If they don't participate, your system will starve on bad inputs and die quietly in "pilot purgatory."

Change management for high-performing commercial teams follows a different rule than most corporate transformation:

**The field does not want to be trained. The field wants to be proven.**

## The Rep Enrollment Playbook

### Move 1: Co-Design the "Approved Lanes" (Not the UI)

Most organizations involve reps too late. They ask for feedback after the system is already defined. That's not co-design. That's blame distribution.

Real co-design focuses on authority boundaries:

- What can the system do without asking?
- What must always escalate?
- What will never be automated because it is identity-defining?

This is where you neutralize identity threat: you show, in writing, that the system is not coming for the parts of the job that create status—trust, negotiation, strategy—while it aggressively removes clerical orchestration.

Adoption guidance consistently recommends involving frontline employees in adoption and pilot design to reduce resistance and increase ownership [https://smartdev.com/ai-use-cases-in-sales/] [https://www.arionresearch.com/blog/6dp61m5njr1rphynbldc1ov2p5a2n8].

### Move 2: Run Small Pilots With Reps Who Have Credibility (Then Make the Results Unavoidable)

Sales organizations don't change through memos. They change through stories—specifically, stories told by the people other reps respect.

The SuperAGI case framing is directionally correct: skepticism was reduced via small-group pilots, training, and metrics-led ROI proof points, including reported outcomes like 30% efficiency gain, 25% lead increase, and 30% cycle reduction [https://web.superagi.com/from-hype-to-reality-real-world-case-studies-of-ai-agents-in-sales-success-stories-2025/].

The structure matters more than the numbers:

- Pick a pilot cohort that includes respected top performers and respected skeptics.
- Instrument baseline metrics before the pilot begins.
- Make the comparison public: time recovered, cycle compression, leakage reduced.

If you cannot produce measurable delta, you should not scale. Not because AI is hard. Because your operating model is still misaligned.

### Move 3: Build a Clear Benefit Path: "What Work Disappears on Day 1?"

Most rollouts promise "insights." Reps don't need more insight. They need less drag.

The benefit path should be written as workload subtraction:

- Which parts of prospecting become automatic?
- Which follow-ups stop requiring memory?
- Which CRM updates stop consuming selling hours?
- Which internal handoffs stop requiring Slack chasing?

This is the tool overload antidote: the new system must remove at least as much surface area as it adds. Practical guidance in the field emphasizes that adoption improves when AI reduces manual work and reps are trained to delegate routine execution to the system, with guardrails to preserve trust [https://fluint.io/post/ai-sales-agents-101-what-they-are-why-you-need-one].

If the first rep experience is "another tab," you are done. If the first rep experience is "I got my afternoon back," you have a chance.

### Move 4: Training Is Not Education. It's Trust Manufacturing.

Sales training fails when it is treated as information transfer. In an agentic system, training has one job: establish when the system is reliable and when it must escalate.

That means training must cover:

- **How the system decides** (inputs, thresholds, constraints).
- **What it will never do** (protected human decision rights).

- **How to override** (the rep's ability to stop or redirect action).
- **How to improve it** (what feedback changes the machine).

This aligns with adoption recommendations emphasizing training and support to build confidence, reduce fear, and prevent resistance rooted in knowledge gaps [https://smartdev.com/ai-use-cases-in-sales/] [https://www.salesloft.com/resources/blog/ai-for-sales] [https://www.arionresearch.com/blog/6dp61m5njr1rphynbldc1ov2p5a2n8].

A rep who knows how to supervise the system stops feeling replaced. They start feeling promoted.

### Move 5: Redesign Incentives Around AI-Augmented Outcomes (Not Activity, Not Usage)

This is where leadership usually fails. They keep compensation and performance management anchored to the old operating model: more activity, more meetings, more logged tasks. Then they wonder why reps treat the new system as theater.

If you want governed autonomy, you pay for what governed autonomy produces:

- **Cycle compression** in defined segments.

- **Leakage reduction** (fewer stalled deals, fewer missed follow-ups).
- **Coverage expansion** without headcount expansion.
- **Forecast integrity** (cleaner evidence, fewer end-of-quarter surprises).

Do not pay for "tool usage." That's how you manufacture resentment and falsified compliance. Pay for outcomes that require human judgment plus system throughput.

## Elaborating the Real-World Cases: What Actually Changed

### IBM Watson (as referenced in sales AI deployment summaries): Proof Came From Time Recovered

Reported examples cite IBM Watson reducing research time by ~50% and improving conversions by ~20% in sales contexts [https://smartdev.com/ai-use-cases-in-sales/].

The structural takeaway isn't "Watson is smart." It's that the first win came from removing a specific rep burden—information gathering—so human hours could move up-stack into judgment and conversations.

That's how adoption begins: the rep experiences reclaimed capacity, not abstract intelligence.

### SuperAGI: Skepticism Collapsed When ROI Was Measured, Not Claimed

The SuperAGI story describes the practical adoption sequence: small pilots, training, iterative refinement, and ROI metrics that made the performance change defensible, with reported outcomes including ~30% efficiency gains, ~25% lead increases, and ~30% cycle reduction [https://web.superagi.com/from-hype-to-reality-real-world-case-studies-of-ai-agents-in-sales-success-stories-2025/].

This is the correct pattern for high-performing sales teams:

- Prove it on real deals.
- Let credible reps narrate the delta.
- Then scale with governance, not enthusiasm.

### Salesforce/Oracle (as referenced in adoption summaries): "Enterprise AI" Worked Where It Attached to Workflows

Summaries of enterprise deployments point to outcomes when AI is attached to concrete workflows—conversion lifts, research-time reductions, and process acceleration—rather than layered as optional advice [https://smartdev.com/ai-use-cases-in-sales/].

This matters because it clarifies the adoption requirement: reps don't adopt "intelligence." They adopt workflow removal.

### Salesloft's Framing: Resistance Drops When Support is Operational, Not Inspirational

Salesloft notes the reality most leaders try to ignore: sales teams resist change, and adoption improves with clear communication, support, and tangible benefit demonstrations—particularly in areas like prospecting, insights, and forecasting where the system can reduce admin load and improve prioritization [https://www.salesloft.com/resources/blog/ai-for-sales].

This is not about messaging. It is about reducing exposure. Reps engage when the system makes performance more controllable, not when it makes evaluation more opaque.

### Fluint: Tool Overload and Data Errors Are Adoption Killers—Unless You Engineer Delegation + Guardrails

Fluint captures the common failure mode: AI tools add noise rather than subtract work, and data errors destroy trust fast. It also points to the necessary redesign: train reps to delegate routine work to agents, and build guardrails so outputs are dependable enough to act on [https://fluint.io/post/ai-sales-agents-101-what-they-are-why-you-need-one].

That is the architecture principle in human terms: when the system is safe to delegate to, reps stop resisting and start reallocating effort into higher-trust work.

## What Executives Must Stop Doing

### Stop Treating Resistance as a Cultural Defect

Resistance is usually an integrity signal:

- the system doesn't reduce workload,
- the data doesn't support action,
- or the organisation is attempting to move authority without control surfaces.

Fix the architecture and resistance drops. Blame the reps and resistance becomes policy.

### Stop Scaling Before You Have a "Trustable Loop"

If you scale autonomy before you can show:

- what actions changed,

- what outcomes improved,
- what errors occurred,
- and how fast you can roll back,

you're not transforming the revenue system. You're running a distributed experiment on your brand and pipeline.

### Stop Adding Tools When the Real Need Is Workload Subtraction

Reps don't resist because they're stubborn. They resist because the stack keeps demanding attention. Tool overload is not solved by better training. It is solved by deleting work.

## The Executive Design Principle: Adoption Is an Outcome of System Credibility

High-performing reps are not "change averse." They are performance accountable. They will accept any system that:

- reduces their workload,
- increases their control over outcomes,
- and preserves their identity as judgment carriers.

This is why the playbook works:

- **Co-design** neutralizes identity threat by making authority boundaries explicit.
- **Clear benefit paths** neutralize tool overload by subtracting work immediately.
- **Pilots + metrics** neutralize data distrust by proving reliability on real deals.
- **New success stories** convert skepticism into social proof from credible peers.
- **Incentive redesign** aligns behavior with the new operating model rather than rewarding the old one.

## The Inevitable Implication: The Companies That Win Will Turn Reps Into System Designers

As agentic revenue systems mature, sales organizations will split into two species.

- **Species one** treats reps as end-users. It rolls out tools, mandates usage, and manages adoption as compliance. It will get friction, workarounds, and slow decay in trust.

- **Species two** treats reps as co-architects of execution authority. It redesigns workflows, proves workload subtraction, and pays for AI-augmented outcomes. It will get cleaner data, faster loops, and calmer quarters.

The second group won't "win because AI." They will win because they built a revenue operating system that the field is willing to live inside. That is the only adoption that scales.

Chapter 17

# The Economics of Autonomy: ROI, Risk, and Payback

## The Board Is Not Asking, "Is AI Real?"

They already know it is.

They are asking something more clinical:

- Does this change our unit economics?
- Does this reduce revenue volatility?
- Does this scale without scaling headcount?
- Does this create a defensible advantage, or just new spend?

Most "AI business cases" fail because they argue for tools. Boards do not fund tools. They fund operating capabilities.

Autonomy is an operating capability. And it has a different economic profile than incremental tooling.

## The Core Distinction: Tool ROI vs. System ROI

Tools promise localized efficiency. A little time saved here. A better email there.

Autonomy changes the throughput of the revenue machine. It compresses cycle time, expands coverage, improves conversion reliability, and reallocates management attention away from arbitration.

That is why autonomy returns are rarely linear. They come from second-order effects:

- **Cycle time compression** reduces cost of carry and increases revenue velocity.
- **Leakage reduction** prevents silent deaths that never show up as “lost.”
- **Coverage expansion** raises baseline execution across the long tail of accounts.
- **Management leverage** increases the span of control without turning leaders into approval clerks.

If you measure autonomy with “hours saved,” you will underfund it. If you measure it with system economics, the case becomes hard to unsee.

## The CFO-Grade Frame: One Model, Four Value Pools

A CFO-grade business case does not begin with features. It begins with a ledger of value pools and a disciplined method for claiming them.

Autonomous execution produces four value pools. Most companies only count one.

### Value Pool 1: Throughput (Revenue Lift)

This is the cleanest board story: more conversion, faster cycles, better expansion capture.

Case evidence is already pointing to the same shape of impact: win-rate lift and cycle compression come from continuous deal monitoring, earlier intervention, and orchestrated follow-through—not from prettier analytics. Zams reports outcomes including a 4% revenue leakage reduction, $775K unlocked in specific deployments, and large time savings (e.g., 4,160 hours), alongside forecasting accuracy improvements from ~60–70% to ~85–95% in cited cases [https://zams.com/blog/agentic-automation-in-action-enterprise-case-studies-that-prove-roi].

Note what those metrics imply economically:

- Leakage reduction is revenue without new demand.
- Forecast accuracy is not "planning quality." It is capital allocation quality.
- Hours saved are only valuable if redeployed into late-stage judgment.

### Value Pool 2: Cost (Labor and Tooling Substitution)

Cost savings in autonomy are real, but they are not the main event. They are the enabling condition: removing coordination work so humans move up the stack.

CX deployments show large-scale savings and ROI profiles that boards recognize because they look like operational redesign, not software experimentation. CX Today highlights examples including Loop's reported 357% ROI, RCBC's savings quantified at 22M, and payback timelines often described in the 12–18 month range for AI agent deployments that reduce cost while lifting revenue [https://www.cxtoday.com/ai-automation-in-cx/ai-agent-roi-growth-automation/].

The CFO translation is straightforward: cost savings are credible when tied to a measurable reduction in manual queue work and rework—then to verified staffing avoidance. Not "productivity." Avoided cost.

### Value Pool 3: Risk (Loss Avoidance and Control)

Risk is where most autonomy cases are weakest—because leaders treat risk as narrative. CFOs treat it as expected value.

Autonomy reduces risk when it creates:

- **lower error rates** in high-frequency execution,

- **faster detection** of degradation before it becomes a miss,
- **auditability** for decisions and actions,
- **suppression** of harmful outreach and operational collisions.

The tight way to quantify risk is not "we will be safer." It is:

- reduced compliance incidents,
- reduced rework cost,
- reduced churn or delay attributable to preventable failures,
- reduction in revenue variance (forecast error bands tighten).

### Value Pool 4: Leverage (Management and Scale)

Leverage is the part boards care about most and teams measure least.

Management leverage is the ability to run more execution volume without:

- more headcount,
- more meetings,
- more approvals,

- or more tool sprawl.

That leverage shows up in enterprise ROI narratives as "scalability without staffing" and "faster payback" because it changes the constraint. The CX examples explicitly frame AI agents as a growth-and-scale mechanism, not a service efficiency tactic, with payback often cited inside 12–18 months [https://www.cxtoday.com/ai-automation-in-cx/ai-agent-roi-growth-automation/].

## Stop Asking for Budget. Start Asking for an Autonomy Envelope.

Most initiatives die because they are pitched as a lump-sum platform buy. That triggers a predictable CFO response: "prove it first."

The correct economic structure is an autonomy envelope: a staged investment plan where authority expands only as verification expands.

This is common in autonomous physical systems because it is the only responsible way to predict payback under uncertainty. OTTO Motors describes business-case construction for autonomous mobile robots using a full cost model (hardware, software, integration, training, maintenance) combined with savings and payback logic, supported by simulation to estimate performance accurately; the article cites examples such as 16-month payback outcomes and large annual savings (e.g., $1.3M/year in a GE example) as the style of justification leaders can defend [https://ottomotors.com/blog/estimating-roi-for-amr-business-case/].

Steal the economic discipline, not the domain:

- Model costs end-to-end, including governance and monitoring.
- Simulate throughput outcomes before scaling authority.
- Release autonomy in approved lanes with measurable limits.
- Expand only when performance and control remain stable.

That is how autonomy becomes fundable. Because it becomes containable.

## The CFO Model: Baseline → Delta → Attribution → Payback

CFOs do not debate strategy. They debate attribution. If you cannot attribute deltas to mechanisms, your ROI will be treated as coincidence.

A CFO-grade model is a four-step construct:

### Step 1: Establish the Baseline (What Is True Today)

- Median cycle length by segment and motion
- Stage-to-stage conversion rates
- Win rate by deal size and source
- Pipeline leakage (stalls, no-decision, timeouts)
- Coverage ratios (accounts touched meaningfully per period)
- Manager bandwidth allocation (time spent on arbitration vs. coaching vs. strategy)

### Step 2: Define the Delta (What Changes Under Governed Autonomy)

Autonomy deltas should be expressed in four board-legible forms:

- **Revenue:** win-rate lift, expansion capture, leakage reduction
- **Time:** cycle compression, time-to-first-response, time-to-next-step
- **Cost:** FTE hours reclaimed, staffing avoidance, reduced rework
- **Risk:** incident reduction, error-rate reduction, variance reduction

### Step 3: Prove Attribution (Why the Delta Occurred)

Attribution comes from instrumentation. Not from rep surveys.

This is where phased deployments and dashboards matter. Samta describes AI case studies emphasizing staged payback windows (often 12–18 months) and measurable operational impacts tied to cycle time improvements and "coverage" style metrics across workflows—exactly the instrumentation pattern required to defend investment decisions without relying on stories [https://samta.ai/blogs/ai-case-studies-that].

### Step 4: Compute Payback (Not Just ROI)

Boards love ROI. CFOs love payback. Because payback exposes whether benefits are real or delayed into fiction.

In the reported enterprise pattern, payback windows for well-scoped autonomy programs often land inside 6–18 months with multi-x returns when the deployment targets execution bottlenecks rather than adding optional tooling layers [https://www.cxtoday.com/ai-automation-in-cx/ai-agent-roi-growth-automation/] [https://zams.com/blog/agentic-automation-in-action-enterprise-case-studies-that-prove-roi] [https://samta.ai/blogs/ai-case-studies-that] [https://wearenotch.com/blog/ai-roi-case-studies/].

## The Metrics That Matter: Four Numbers That Make Autonomy Legible

If you want the board to fund autonomy, you must stop reporting activity. Report system performance.

### Metric 1: Cycle Time Compression

Cycle time compression is not a sales productivity metric. It is a capital efficiency metric. Shorter cycles reduce pipeline carry cost, reduce end-of-quarter discounting pressure, and increase revenue velocity.

Zams' case examples explicitly quantify time savings and cycle-related benefits as a primary ROI driver (including large hour reductions) because time is the container of revenue throughput [https://zams.com/blog/agentic-automation-in-action-enterprise-case-studies-that-prove-roi].

### Metric 2: Coverage Ratio

Coverage ratio answers a brutal question: "What percentage of the book receives high-quality follow-through without heroics?"

Autonomy's first structural win is raising the baseline across the long tail. Samta's discussion of coverage-style metrics and workflow automation outcomes shows this as a recurring enterprise measurement pattern: value is measured by how much of the operational surface becomes reliably executed, not by how impressive the model is in a demo [https://samta.ai/blogs/ai-case-studies-that].

### Metric 3: Win-Rate Lift (By Regime)

Win-rate lift must be tracked by regime: segment, deal size, source, motion type. Otherwise, you hide failure inside averages and call it progress.

Zams' cited improvements include win-rate-related outcomes tied to deal monitoring and pipeline intelligence—because deals stop silently degrading when a system defends them continuously [https://zams.com/blog/agentic-automation-in-action-enterprise-case-studies-that-prove-roi].

### Metric 4: Management Leverage

Management leverage is the ratio of:

- execution surface area supervised
- to human managerial attention required

It is the hidden economic lever because it is where growth usually starts to choke.

Notch's ROI case roundup emphasizes leverage patterns—time saved per employee, scaled benefits, and large productivity improvements—often presented as the real reason AI programs keep funding: they change how much output the organization can carry without proportional staffing [https://wearenotch.com/blog/ai-roi-case-studies/].

## The Autonomy Value Dashboard: One Page the CFO Will Actually Use

Dashboards usually fail because they are descriptive. This one is evaluative. It answers: is autonomy creating value faster than it is creating risk?

### Panel A: Throughput

- Revenue velocity (by segment)
- Cycle length (median, not just average)
- Stage conversion rates (with leading indicators)
- Leakage rate (timeouts, no-decision, stalled-state duration)

### Panel B: Coverage

- % accounts receiving "baseline good execution" per week
- % opportunities with mapped buying group minimum
- % opportunities with verified next step inside SLA

### Panel C: Leverage

- Manager intervention rate (exceptions per 100 opportunities)
- Exception packet quality (time-to-resolution, re-escalation rate)
- Headcount avoided (validated through output stability, not intent)

### Panel D: Risk and Control

- Policy blocks (attempted actions blocked by constraints)
- Rollback events (count, cause, time-to-contain)
- Compliance incidents (trend, severity)
- Customer fatigue indicators (suppression triggers, opt-out spikes)

## The Real Cost Model: Autonomy Is Not Software. It Is an Operating Capability.

If you cost autonomy like a tool, you will underestimate it and then declare it "underperforming."

A real cost model includes:

- **Build and integration:** workflow wiring, event streams, canonical data enforcement
- **Governance:** approved lanes, policy constraints, auditability, rollback drills
- **Monitoring:** drift, anomalies, suppression, exception routing
- **Operating labor:** RevOps as control engineering, not reporting
- **Change load:** role redesign and incentive alignment

OTTO Motors' AMR business case structure is useful precisely because it forces full-cost visibility: hardware/software is not the main cost; deployment, training, and operational design are what determine payback credibility—and simulations are used to prevent fantasy projections [https://ottomotors.com/blog/estimating-roi-for-amr-business-case/].

Revenue autonomy deserves the same seriousness. Not because it is heavy. Because it is consequential.

## Risk Is Not an Objection. It Is a Value Stream.

Most executives treat risk controls as the tax you pay to get autonomy approved. CFOs want the opposite framing: risk reduction is part of the return.

CX deployments often justify agents through risk and compliance improvements alongside savings and revenue lift—because fewer errors and better consistency are measurable outcomes, not philosophical benefits [https://www.cxtoday.com/ai-automation-in-cx/ai-agent-roi-growth-automation/].

In revenue, the risk ledger includes:

- misrouted accounts and territory conflicts
- duplicated outreach and brand inconsistency
- unapproved claims and compliance exposure
- discount corridor violations and margin drift
- forecast volatility that drives reactive spending

Autonomy reduces these when governance is designed as a mechanism, not a memo.

## The Payback Pattern: Why It's Often Fast When It's Real

Autonomy payback is fast when it attacks execution latency and coordination drag. Those costs are already present. They are simply hidden in human time and quarter-end concessions.

Zams' cases quantify leak reduction and time reclaimed; CX Today reports ROI and savings cases with 12–18 month paybacks; Notch aggregates enterprise examples that emphasize scaled returns and productivity improvements; Samta describes staged enterprise outcomes and payback framing [https://zams.com/blog/agentic-automation-in-action-enterprise-case-studies-that-prove-roi] [https://www.cxtoday.com/ai-automation-in-cx/ai-agent-roi-growth-automation/] [https://wearenotch.com/blog/ai-roi-case-studies/] [https://samta.ai/blogs/ai-case-studies-that].

The consistent shape is not "AI magic." It is structural: remove waiting, remove rework, prevent silent decay, and redeploy human judgment to the few moments that decide outcomes.

## The Investment Defense: How to Speak to the Board Without Selling Fiction

Boards will ask the same three questions every time:

- What is the mechanism of return?
- What are the failure modes?
- What is our control plan?

Your defense is not enthusiasm. It is architecture plus instrumentation.

Use this board narrative:

- **We are not buying AI tools.** We are redesigning execution loops.
- **We will start with one reference circuit** and instrument baseline vs. delta.
- **We will expand authority only inside approved lanes** with audit, rollback, and suppression.
- **We will report the autonomy value dashboard monthly** until performance is stable enough to move to quarterly governance.

- **We will hold payback to a defined window** and kill or contain initiatives that do not show measurable delta.

That is how autonomy becomes investable. Because it becomes governable.

## The Inevitable Implication: The New Unit of Efficiency Is Not the Rep. It Is the Loop.

Incremental tooling optimizes people. Autonomy redesigns loops.

The board-level outcome is predictable:

- Companies that measure "AI adoption" will accumulate spend and stories.
- Companies that measure loop economics will compound throughput, predictability, and leverage.

In the next era, ROI will not be credited to who bought the smartest software. It will be credited to who built the most disciplined execution system—and could prove it with numbers that survive audit.

Chapter 18

# Why Most AI Pilots Stall — and How to Break Through

## The Pilot Is Not a Phase. It's a Graveyard.

Most "AI pilots" don't fail. They fossilize.

They get labeled "promising." Then they get parked. A new cohort is launched next quarter. Another demo lands. Another internal update deck gets made. And nothing structural changes in the operating model.

Leaders call this experimentation. It isn't. It's avoidance.

A pilot that cannot graduate is not learning. It is the organization admitting—quietly—that it cannot absorb execution authority into the system.

This chapter is about the real reason pilots stall:

- Not because the capability doesn't exist.
- Because the organization didn't design a path to production.

## The Four Failure Patterns That Create "Sandbox Purgatory"

### Failure Pattern 1: Sandbox Purgatory (The Pilot Was Never Designed to Become Real)

Sandbox purgatory is a pilot built for demonstration, not deployment. It looks functional in a lab environment, then collapses when it touches real workflows, real data, real incentives, and real accountability.

This is why the "95% fail" narrative persists: pilots start with excitement, then die on contact with production reality—data readiness, adoption friction, and integration complexity [https://trullion.com/blog/why-95-of-ai-projects-fail-and-why-the-5-that-survive-matter/] [https://www.congruity360.com/blog/why-95-of-generative-ai-pilots-are-failing/].

Executives misread this as a technology problem. It's an architecture problem: the pilot does not have a production lane. So it stays in the sandbox. Forever.

## Failure Pattern 2: No Clear Owner (So the Pilot Has No Right to Exist)

In most organizations, pilots are "owned" the way committees are owned. Everyone is involved. No one is accountable.

That creates the predictable outcome: the pilot survives as an initiative, not as a capability. Because capabilities require one person with the power to make trade-offs: scope, data access, workflow impact, governance, and rollout sequencing.

A real-world counterexample is instructive: an NHS Trust built an explicit implementation and governance framework that assigned multi-stakeholder roles—clinical lead, CIO, safety, and others—inside a structured plan, including benefits realization and risk management, with phased rollout patterns like silent-mode testing [https://www.digitalregulations.innovation.nhs.uk/case-studies/setting-up-an-implementation-and-governance-framework-for-artificial-intelligence-ai-pilot-studies-taking-place-in-an-nhs-trust/pdf/].

Steal the mechanism, not the setting: ownership is not a name on a slide. Ownership is governance with decision rights.

### Failure Pattern 3: Weak Success Criteria (So "Good" Becomes a Story)

Most pilot KPIs are designed to be unkillable:

- "Improve productivity."
- "Increase pipeline quality."
- "Reduce admin time."
- "Enhance customer experience."

These are not success criteria. They are aspirations. A pilot measured with aspirations becomes a narrative contest. And narrative contests do not graduate into core operations.

The Cloud Security Alliance's guidance is blunt about what breaks this pattern: pilots should start with clear objectives and measurable KPIs, prioritizing high-impact, low-risk use cases with data readiness and governance to bridge to enterprise adoption [https://cloudsecurityalliance.org/blog/2025/03/28/a-guide-on-how-ai-pilot-programs-are-shaping-enterprise-adoption].

Success criteria must be mechanical: something that can be verified without interpretation. If you can't measure it cleanly, you can't scale it safely.

### Failure Pattern 4: Misaligned Incentives (So Production Is Nobody's Win)

Pilots often live inside innovation teams, data teams, or enthusiastic operators. Production lives inside the business.

When those incentive structures are misaligned, a pilot can be "successful" and still never ship:

- The pilot team gets rewarded for demos and novelty.
- The operating team gets punished for disruption, risk, and added workload.
- Leadership gets stories, not throughput.

This is why pilots so often stall "in labs," even when the output is impressive [https://trullion.com/blog/why-95-of-ai-projects-fail-and-why-the-5-that-survive-matter/].

A pilot graduates when production is the incentive—not the burden. That requires executive air cover: explicit permission to change workflow, reallocate time, and force cross-functional cooperation. Without it, pilots remain optional. Optional doesn't scale.

## The Structural Reframe: A Pilot Is a Production Design Exercise

Most organizations run pilots like experiments. The organizations that break through run pilots like operating model tests.

A pilot is not "Can the model do it?" A pilot is:

**Can we make this governable inside our revenue operating system?**

That means a pilot has to prove four things simultaneously:

- **Execution value**: does it change outcomes, not outputs?
- **Integration viability**: can it run inside real workflows, not beside them?
- **Governance containment**: can we permission, audit, and roll back behavior?
- **Organizational absorption**: will the field actually use it because it subtracts work?

## The Breakthrough Method: The Pilot Graduation Ladder

To break out of sandbox purgatory, you need a ladder that forces graduation conditions. Not encouragement. Conditions.

### Step 1: Choose a Use Case That Is High-Impact *and* Narrow

Most pilots fail because leaders pick a broad use case ("improve sales productivity") that feels strategic, then discover it is ungovernable. The survivors pick a narrow problem that sits inside a real workflow and can be measured precisely.

This is echoed in the pilot best-practice framing: prioritize high-impact, low-risk use cases with clear metrics and readiness, then expand from verified performance [https://cloudsecurityalliance.org/blog/2025/03/28/a-guide-on-how-ai-pilot-programs-are-shaping-enterprise-adoption].

Trullion's analysis points to the same survival trait: the projects that last tend to be niche and workflow-integrated, not generic "AI everywhere" initiatives [https://trullion.com/blog/why-95-of-ai-projects-fail-and-why-the-5-that-survive-matter/].

If the use case cannot be expressed as a bounded circuit—signal → decision → action → outcome—it is not a pilot. It is exploration. Exploration has its place. It should not be confused with production progress.

### Step 2: Assign a Single Executive Owner With the Power to Ship

Ownership is a design decision. The owner must have:

- authority to change workflow,
- access rights to required data,
- control over resources,
- and political leverage to resolve cross-functional conflict.

The NHS governance case shows why: pilots were framed with strategic alignment, role clarity, risk management, and phased adoption—creating a path from evaluation to implementation rather than leaving translation to chance [https://www.digitalregulations.innovation.nhs.uk/case-studies/setting-up-an-implementation-and-governance-framework-for-artificial-intelligence-ai-pilot-studies-taking-place-in-an-nhs-trust/pdf/].

Do not delegate the pilot to the "AI team." If the system is supposed to run revenue execution, then revenue leadership must own it. Not cheerlead it. Own it.

### Step 3: Establish "Killable" Success Criteria Before the First Build

A pilot with unkillable criteria becomes political. A pilot with killable criteria becomes operational.

Use success criteria in three tiers:

- **Outcome metric** (board-legible): cycle time, conversion, leakage reduction, forecast error band tightening.
- **Mechanism metric** (operator-legible): latency reduction, exception rate, loop closure rate, coverage increase.
- **Control metric** (risk-legible): policy violations blocked, audit trail completeness, rollback time-to-contain.

CSA's adoption guidance emphasizes the necessity of clear objectives and metrics to avoid pilots becoming directionless experiments [https://cloudsecurityalliance.org/blog/2025/03/28/a-guide-on-how-ai-pilot-programs-are-shaping-enterprise-adoption].

If you cannot define the kill conditions, you are not piloting. You are sponsoring a pet project.

### Step 4: Build the Pilot Inside Governance, Not Beside It

The most common pilot lie is "we'll add governance later." Later never arrives. Later is where pilots go to die.

Congruity360's diagnosis highlights why pilots fail at scale: data quality and inconsistency create brittleness, and pilots that ignore integration and alignment don't survive production requirements [https://www.congruity360.com/blog/why-95-of-generative-ai-pilots-are-failing/].

A pilot must include:

- explicit permissions (what it can access and do),
- auditability (what happened and why),
- exception handling (when it escalates),
- and rollback (how fast you can stop it).

If you skip governance, you don't get speed. You get one incident and a shutdown.

### Step 5: Require a Production Implementation Plan as the Output

The pilot is not complete when the model works. The pilot is complete when you have a step-by-step production plan with cost, timeline, operating ownership, and rollout sequencing.

Duke Corporate Education's "AI Factory" approach is a useful structural pattern here: use-case gathering, business analysis, feasibility assessment, then POC development—designed to produce implementation plans rather than orphaned demos [https://www.dukece.com/insights/make-your-ai-pilot-a-success/].

Their UK government agency example is revealing precisely because it wasn't "cool AI." It was disciplined execution: executive training, scoped pilots, and a reported 60% acceleration in automation—because the pilots were engineered to become real [https://www.dukece.com/insights/make-your-ai-pilot-a-success/].

In a revenue organization, the output of a pilot should be:

- the operating lane it will live in,

- the workflows it will touch end-to-end,
- the roles it will change,
- the governance mechanisms that contain it,
- and the metrics that will be reported during scaled rollout.

If your pilot ends with "next we'll explore...," you didn't pilot. You marketed internally.

## The "Graduation Gate": The Four Proofs Required Before You Scale

Pilots should not be scaled by enthusiasm. They should be scaled by proofs.

### Proof 1: Workflow Attachment

The capability must be embedded in the workflow it is supposed to change. If it requires a separate tool, separate logins, or separate behavior rituals, it will remain optional—and adoption will decay.

Surviving projects are typically those that integrate tightly into specific workflows rather than operating as vague, general intelligence layers [https://trullion.com/blog/why-95-of-ai-projects-fail-and-why-the-5-that-survive-matter/].

### Proof 2: Data Viability Under Real Conditions

A pilot must prove it can operate on the data you actually have. Not the data you wish you had.

Data insufficiency and inconsistency are repeatedly cited drivers of pilot failure and post-pilot collapse [https://www.congruity360.com/blog/why-95-of-generative-ai-pilots-are-failing/].

This is why pilots must include data-readiness checks as a first-class requirement, not a late-stage discovery [https://cloudsecurityalliance.org/blog/2025/03/28/a-guide-on-how-ai-pilot-programs-are-shaping-enterprise-adoption].

### Proof 3: Control Surfaces

A pilot must prove it can be governed: permissioned, auditable, constrained, reversible.

The NHS case's phased and governance-forward approach is a blueprint: governance and safety are not wrappers; they are prerequisites for real-world operation [https://www.digitalregulations.innovation.nhs.uk/case-studies/setting-up-an-implementation-and-governance-framework-for-artificial-intelligence-ai-pilot-studies-taking-place-in-an-nhs-trust/pdf/].

### Proof 4: Economic Delta

You do not scale a pilot because it is interesting. You scale it because it changes throughput.

That requires baseline vs. delta measurement tied to a real business metric and sustained long enough to rule out noise—exactly the KPI discipline emphasized in enterprise pilot-to-adoption guidance [https://cloudsecurityalliance.org/blog/2025/03/28/a-guide-on-how-ai-pilot-programs-are-shaping-enterprise-adoption].

## The Executive Requirement: "Air Cover" Is Not Support. It's Authority.

Leaders love to say they "support" pilots. Support is cheap. Air cover is expensive.

Air cover means:

- You force cross-functional cooperation when incentives clash.
- You protect the team when pilot outputs create political discomfort.
- You allow workflow disruption in service of a better operating model.

- You fund the integration and governance work, not just the prototype.

Duke CE's executive training emphasis matters because it addresses the real constraint: executives have to understand what they are authorizing, not just what they are buying [https://www.dukece.com/insights/make-your-ai-pilot-a-success/].

Without executive air cover, pilots become side quests. With it, they become operating model migrations.

## The One Rule That Ends Pilot Purgatory

Most pilots are designed to prove capability. That is why they stall.

Design to prove **graduation**.

A graduation-designed pilot has:

- one owner,
- one bounded workflow circuit,
- one set of killable success criteria,
- one governance lane,
- one production plan as the output.

That design moves the organization from curiosity to commitment. And commitment is the only thing that produces structural advantage.

## The Inevitable Implication: Organizations Won't Separate by Models. They'll Separate by Graduation Capability.

Nearly everyone can pilot. Very few can graduate.

That will become the dividing line in the next era of revenue execution:

- Some companies will keep running pilots as theater—accumulating demos, costs, and internal fatigue.
- Others will treat pilots as production gates—earning governed autonomy one lane at a time.

The second group will not look more innovative. They will look more controlled. And in an era where execution authority is moving into the system, control is the entire game.

Do you want to stay ahead of the wave?

The Agentic Revenue Brief

by Tim Cortinovis

How revenue leaders build autonomous execution engines — before their competitors do

Weekly clarity for **CROs, VPs Sales,** and **RevOps** leaders under pressure to deliver growth without adding headcount.

**Get the free Friday Brief**

**https://www.timcortinovis.com/tarb**

High-signal insights on autonomous revenue systems. No hype. No vendor fluff.

Your pipeline looks busy. Your forecast feels fragile. Your reps are drowning in tools.

AI is everywhere. Clarity is not.

Chapter 19

# Aligning Sales, RevOps, Marketing, and Compliance

## The First Thing Autonomy Breaks Is Your Org Chart

Most revenue organizations are not built to execute. They're built to negotiate.

Sales negotiates with Marketing over lead quality.

Marketing negotiates with RevOps over attribution.

RevOps negotiates with Finance over definitions.

Compliance negotiates with everyone after something ships.

In the manual era, this was inefficient but survivable. Humans absorbed the friction. Meetings acted as middleware. Top performers patched the gaps.

Autonomous execution removes the buffer.

The moment your system can detect, decide, and act continuously, functional silos stop being an organizational nuisance and become an execution failure mode. Not because people are uncooperative. Because autonomy can't route through politics. It routes through architecture.

This is the structural shift:

- **Old world:** cross-functional alignment is a leadership skill.
- **New world:** cross-functional alignment is a runtime property of the revenue system.

## Why Silos Kill Autonomous Execution (Quietly, Then Suddenly)

Silos don't just slow decisions. They create conflicting authorities.

An agentic system cannot safely run when four departments hold four incompatible definitions of "qualified," "active," "allowed to send," and "safe to claim."

What breaks first is not performance. It's trust.

- Sales stops trusting lead scoring because Marketing changed a definition.
- Marketing stops trusting pipeline feedback because Sales bypassed routing rules.
- RevOps becomes the human translator between dashboards instead of the engineer of execution.

- Compliance becomes the emergency brake, because nobody designed brakes into the system.

Then performance breaks. Because the system starts executing contradictions at scale.

## The New Alignment Unit: The Revenue Loop, Not the Function

Aligning functions is the wrong goal. Functions are not where revenue happens. Revenue happens in loops:

- **Signal → Decision → Action → Outcome → Learning**

Autonomy makes the loop continuous. Which means alignment must also become continuous. Not as an all-hands meeting. As an operating design.

The winning organizations stop asking, "How do we get Marketing and Sales aligned?" They ask, "How do we create one governable loop that both inhabit?"

## The Operating Model Shift: From Campaigns and Quarters to Operating Rhythms

Legacy GTM runs on episodic rhythms: monthly campaign planning, weekly pipeline reviews, quarterly forecast theater.

Agentic GTM runs on two rhythms simultaneously:

- **Machine rhythm:** continuous detection and bounded action.
- **Human rhythm:** periodic governance, exception judgment, and system evolution.

If you don't design the human rhythm, the machine rhythm will become political chaos. If you slow the machine rhythm to fit your meetings, you lose the point of autonomy.

### The Four Rhythms of an Aligned Agentic GTM Organization

- **Daily: Exception Triage**
  One cross-functional view of what the system escalated, what it suppressed, and what it needs humans to decide. Not a status meeting. A control meeting.

- **Weekly: Loop Health Review**
  Review system health metrics: latency, leakage, coverage, false positives, suppressions, policy blocks. Decide what to tune.

- **Monthly: Policy + Play Release**
  Versioned changes to plays, permissions, claims libraries, routing rules, and thresholds—shipped as a controlled release, not "enablement updates."

- **Quarterly: Autonomy Boundary Reset**
  Expand or tighten autonomy lanes by segment and action class based on evidence. Treat this like capital allocation, not change management.

These rhythms replace "alignment" with operating cadence. You stop begging functions to coordinate. You force the system to coordinate by design.

## Shared Metrics: The Only Antidote to Local Optimization

Silos persist because metrics reward them. Marketing gets rewarded for volume. Sales gets rewarded for closed-won. RevOps gets rewarded for cleanliness. Compliance gets rewarded for prevention.

None of these metrics measure the thing autonomy changes: system throughput under governance.

Aligned agentic GTM requires a small set of shared metrics that every function is accountable to—because every function is now part of the same execution loop.

### The Five Shared Metrics That Replace Functional Scorecards

- **Signal-to-Action Latency**: how long it takes for a meaningful signal to produce a governed action across the GTM system.
- **Coverage Quality**: % of ICP accounts receiving "baseline good execution" (right touch, right time, no collisions), not just "touched."
- **Leakage Rate**: stalled states, silent no-decisions, handoff drops—measured as system failure, not rep failure.
- **Exception Load**: escalations per 100 accounts/opportunities, plus time-to-resolution. This reveals whether autonomy is governable or noisy.
- **Policy Integrity**: blocks, violations prevented, suppression triggers, rollback events.

Compliance becomes measurable without becoming a bottleneck.

This is what alignment looks like when it's real: everyone optimizes the same loop, not their own dashboard.

## Decision Rights: Stop Pretending "Collaboration" Is a Governance System

Most cross-functional misalignment is not interpersonal. It's constitutional. No one knows who is allowed to decide what.

Autonomy forces the issue because the system needs explicit authority boundaries. If humans can't agree on decision rights, the system will escalate constantly—or act ungoverned.

### The Decision Rights Matrix (What Must Be Explicit)

- **Marketing owns:** signal definitions for engagement events, message library inputs, campaign intent.
- **Sales owns:** account strategy pivots, high-trust outreach, deal-level exceptions the system escalates.

- **RevOps owns:** canonical definitions, routing logic, orchestration workflow integrity, instrumentation, and performance verification.
- **Compliance/Legal owns:** claims constraints, restricted segments, approval thresholds for irreversible commitments, and policy-as-code rules that the system enforces.

Notice the shift: functions keep their expertise. They lose their unilateral execution control. Execution is centralized in the system. Governance is distributed through decision rights.

## The Agentic GTM Council: Governance Without the Drag

Most companies will try to govern autonomous execution with a committee. That guarantees one outcome: autonomy slows until it becomes irrelevant.

The agentic GTM council is not a committee. It is the operating authority for the execution system. Its job is not to "align stakeholders." Its job is to keep autonomy fast, safe, and compounding.

### What the Council Governs (And What It Must Never Touch)

- **Governs:** autonomy boundaries, approved lanes, policy constraints, shared metrics, exception thresholds, release cadence, rollback drills.
- **Does not govern:** deal-by-deal decisions, ad hoc campaign tweaks, rep coaching, or "approval of AI outputs." That's how councils become speed killers.

### Composition: A Small Room With Real Authority

A functional council is small by design:

- CRO (execution outcome owner)
- Head of RevOps (control engineering owner)
- Head of Marketing/Growth (signal + narrative owner)
- Compliance/Legal lead (policy owner)
- Data/Platform owner (operability owner) — title varies, responsibility does not

Salesforce's Agentforce playbook describes governance patterns that include clear ownership, ethical guidelines, and measurement frameworks, supported by the Zota story—scaling from one agent to 30+

across departments while handling 180,000 inquiries [https://www.salesforce.com/au/blog/playbook/agentic-ai/]. The important part is not the agent count. It's cross-functional scale under a defined governance model.

### Operating Rules: How It Avoids Strangling Speed

- **All decisions are lane-based.** If a proposed change doesn't map to a lane, it doesn't ship.
- **All changes are versioned releases.** Plays, policies, thresholds—treated like production.
- **All debates must terminate in instrumentation.** If you can't measure it, you can't govern it.
- **Approvals are reserved for irreversible commitments.** Everything else is constrained by policy and audited after execution.

## Five Field Stories: How Alignment Actually Happens When Autonomy Is Real

These aren't "AI success stories." They're alignment stories—because autonomy forces teams to share workflows, metrics, and control surfaces.

### 1) SuperAGI (EcomPlus): Multi-Agent Orchestration That Collapsed Sales/Marketing Friction

In SuperAGI's GTM case studies, EcomPlus moved from manual, siloed execution to coordinated agents across lead qualification, personalization, and follow-ups—reporting 75% revenue growth and 90% reduction in time spent on emails, achieved via phased rollouts and team involvement [https://web.superagi.com/case-studies-in-agentic-gtm-real-world-examples-of-how-autonomous-ai-agents-boost-sales-and-marketing-efficiency/].

Read the mechanism:

- Qualification stopped being a marketing-to-sales argument and became a shared system behavior.
- Follow-through stopped being rep diligence and became workflow integrity.
- Performance stopped being "which team worked harder" and became "how fast the loop closed."

Phased rollouts matter here because they create a new rhythm: instrument, prove, widen the lane. Alignment emerges as an operating discipline, not a cultural aspiration.

### 2) Boomi: The "Agent Control Tower" as Central Visibility for Distributed Autonomy

Boomi's agentic AI use cases describe an "Agent Control Tower" for centralized monitoring alongside large-scale agent deployment (cited as 33,000+ agents) and include GTM-adjacent examples like lead scoring and campaign automation, with governance controls and reporting patterns shown across functions [https://boomi.com/blog/10-agentic-ai-use-cases/].

This is the council mechanism made visible:

- **Visibility is centralized.** Execution can be distributed, but oversight cannot.
- **Monitoring becomes the enabling constraint.** Without a control tower, autonomy becomes shadow execution.

Most organizations try to "align" by adding meetings. Control towers align by making behavior observable and governable in one place.

### 3) Highspot: Agentic Workflows That Tie Autonomy to Outcomes Under RevOps Governance

Highspot's description of agentic workflows spans Sales, Marketing, and Enablement—out-of-the-box workflows that trigger tasks, prioritize pipeline, and adapt actions contextually, with emphasis on tying agents to outcomes under governance rather than letting automation sprawl into optional suggestions [https://www.highspot.com/blog/agentic-workflows/].

The important shift is structural:

- Enablement stops being a content library and becomes a runtime layer in execution.
- RevOps stops being reporting and becomes orchestration governance.
- Sales stops being the owner of "next step memory" and becomes the owner of exceptions.

This is how silos erode without a reorg. Workflows replace persuasion.

### 4) Salesforce Agentforce (Zota): Scaling Cross-Department Agents With Governance, Not Chaos

Salesforce's Agentforce playbook describes scaling agents through governance—clear ownership, ethical guidelines, and measurement frameworks. The Zota story shows expansion from one agent to 30+ across departments, handling 180,000 inquiries [https://www.salesforce.com/au/blog/playbook/agentic-ai/].

Two lessons matter for revenue leaders:

- **Scaling agents is a governance achievement.** The technical act of adding agents is easy. The organizational act of keeping them coherent is the work.
- **Cross-functional scale forces shared metrics.** You cannot run 30 agents across departments if each department measures success differently. You will manufacture conflict at machine speed.

This is what the agentic GTM council exists to prevent: fast proliferation without shared control.

### 5) Forrester: "Casting" Agent Archetypes to Prevent Siloed Autonomy

Forrester's agent archetypes for B2B GTM emphasize multi-agent "casting" (rule-follower, choreographer, and other roles) across Sales and Marketing workflows, advocating governance and hybrid human-agent decisions with role specialization and accountability [https://www.forrester.com/blogs/meet-the-ai-agents-redefining-b2b-gtm-strategies-and-approaches-at-b2b-summit-emea/].

This matters because it solves a common alignment failure: a single generalized agent becomes the new silo.

Archetypes create a division of labor that mirrors how strong organizations actually work:

- Rule-followers enforce constraints.
- Choreographers coordinate cross-functional sequences.
- Humans arbitrate edge cases and intent shifts.

In other words: you don't just add autonomy. You design a governable society of agents—and you assign humans to govern the constitution, not the everyday traffic.

## The Anti-Pattern Most Companies Will Choose: "Compliance as the Brake Pedal"

When autonomy meets risk, the default enterprise response is predictable: route everything through approvals.

That produces two outcomes:

- Speed dies.
- Shadow autonomy emerges anyway, because the business still needs throughput.

The correct model is not approval-heavy. It is constraint-heavy.

Compliance is not there to review execution. Compliance is there to encode the boundaries execution cannot cross—then monitor drift and incidents.

That is why the agentic GTM council must treat compliance as a design partner, not a gatekeeper. Governance is not an endpoint. Governance is what makes speed survivable.

## The Blueprint: How to Break Silos Without a Reorg

### Move 1: Establish a Single GTM Truth Surface

One set of definitions for:

- ICP and account state
- Lead qualification state
- Opportunity stage evidence
- Suppression states (do-not-contact, procurement active, fatigue)

Without this, every agent is forced to pick a side. And the side it picks becomes your next internal war.

### Move 2: Pick One Cross-Functional Reference Circuit

Not "improve alignment." A circuit.

Example circuits:

- Inbound intent → qualification → routing → first outreach → meeting → opportunity creation
- Opportunity risk signals → intervention → suppression → escalation packet → human decision

Instrument it end-to-end. Govern it. Then expand.

### Move 3: Install the Council With Release Authority

The council's authority must be explicit:

- It owns lane definitions.
- It ships policy and play releases.
- It sets and enforces shared metrics.
- It controls rollback and incident response.

If the council cannot ship, it is a discussion group. Discussion groups don't control autonomous execution. They describe it after it breaks.

### Move 4: Align Incentives to Shared Metrics

Do not pay Marketing for volume if the system is optimizing for coverage quality. Do not pay Sales for close at any cost if the system is enforcing policy integrity. Do not grade RevOps on dashboard uptime if the system is being governed by exception load and latency.

Align incentives to the loop. The loop will align the functions.

## The Inevitable Implication: GTM Will Be Managed Like a Product

This is where the shift ends.

As execution becomes autonomous, GTM stops being a set of departments and becomes a governed system with releases, metrics, control surfaces, and versioned evolution.

The organizations that win will not be the ones with "tight collaboration." They will be the ones with:

- one execution loop,
- one set of shared metrics,
- one decision-rights constitution,

- and one council that can govern evolution without strangling speed.

Everyone else will keep trying to align humans to compensate for an unaligned system.

In the agentic era, the system is the company customers meet. If the system is fragmented, the company is fragmented. And the market will price you accordingly.

Chapter 20

# The VP Sales as System Architect

## The VP of Sales Used to Run the Quarter. Now They Run the Machine.

The old VP Sales job was deal supervision at scale: forecast calls, pipeline interrogation, late-stage escalation, end-of-quarter triage. A human control system trying to keep a fragile revenue engine from rattling apart.

That job is expiring. Not because leadership mattered less. Because the coordination problem has changed shape.

In an agentic revenue organization, the system carries the baseline execution: signal detection, routing, sequencing, follow-through, risk triage, and workflow motion. Once that becomes true, the top commercial leader cannot be the head waiter of deals. They must become the architect of the revenue system.

This is not a title shift. It is a constitutional shift in how revenue is governed.

## The Shift: From "Managing Sellers" to "Designing Execution"

Most VPs of Sales still think their job is to increase performance by managing people. That was rational when the primary production unit was the individual rep.

Autonomy changes the production unit. The new production unit is the loop: signal → decision → action → learning.

So the VP Sales role becomes:

- **Design the loop**, not just motivate the participants.
- **Set decision rights**, not just enforce compliance.
- **Govern autonomy**, not just inspect activity.
- **Build cross-functional execution**, not just cross-functional alignment.

In short: you stop running the quarter as a recurring emergency. You redesign the system so the quarter runs with fewer emergencies.

## The Four Core Competencies of the System Architect VP Sales

### 1) Systems Thinking: Design for Reuse, Not Heroics

The most expensive sales organizations are not the ones with high compensation. They're the ones that pay for the same thinking repeatedly. Every deal re-invents discovery, re-invents solution design, re-invents stakeholder mapping, re-in-invents risk handling.

Systems thinking replaces "best rep behavior" with "institutional behavior." It treats selling as an engineered sequence of states, outputs, constraints, and handoffs.

Vivun's solution-architecture best practices describe sellers operating as architects: designing scalable, reusable solutions, capturing system knowledge centrally, and pressure-testing proposals for edge cases through "Red Team" style testing rather than trusting optimistic narratives [https://www.vivun.com/blog/solution-architecture-best-practices-for-sellers-from-design-to-revenue]. That is exactly the VP Sales posture shift: build mechanisms that survive talent variance.

A system architect VP Sales builds:

- **Reference architectures** for common customer problems.
- **Standard objects** for what "qualified," "validated," and "closed" mean operationally.
- **Execution circuits** that run end-to-end without human middleware.
- **Failure mode libraries** that turn deal losses into system updates, not folklore.

The VP Sales stops asking, "Who can save this deal?" They start asking, "Why did the system allow this deal state to persist?"

### 2) Data Literacy: Not Dashboards. Decision-Grade Evidence.

Data literacy used to mean "understanding the funnel." That's quaint.

In an agentic system, data is not a description. Data is delegated authority. If the system can act, then the inputs must be action-safe: consistent, timely, and auditable.

This is why the VP Sales must be able to read the revenue system the way an operator reads an instrument panel: not for insight, but for control.

Force Management's cross-functional execution framing shows the practical reality: sales execution improves when qualification and messaging are unified across teams through shared methods (e.g., MEDDICC-style rigor) and consistent workflows, extending "sales" beyond the sales team into customer journey coordination [https://www.forcemanagement.com/blog/selling-beyond-the-sales-team-how-a-cross-functional-approach-improves-execution]. That is data literacy as operating discipline: shared definitions that prevent internal contradictions.

The architect VP Sales is literate in:

- **Semantic integrity**: one meaning per term across functions.
- **Signal quality**: which signals drive decisions without creating noise.
- **Coverage reality**: where execution is actually happening vs. being narrated.

- **Exception economics**: what escalates, why it escalates, and how to reduce escalation volume while improving escalation quality.

The correct ambition is not "better reporting." It is fewer moments where leadership must convene a meeting to discover what is true.

### 3) Experimentation: Controlled Change, Not Quarterly Reinvention

Most sales organizations already run experiments. They just call them "new talk tracks." They're uncontrolled, unmeasured, and usually indistinguishable from a mood swing.

Experimentation as a system architect is different: it is the controlled evolution of an execution machine. The goal is not creativity. The goal is verified improvement without destabilizing production.

Vivun's emphasis on rigorous testing for edge cases—explicitly using "Red Team" approaches—points to the maturity required when selling becomes an engineered discipline: you stress-test the solution and messaging before it scales into the field [https://www.vivun.com/blog/solution-architecture-best-practices-for-sellers-from-design-to-revenue]. That is experimentation as governance, not as novelty.

The MIT Sloan case study of computer-aided architects captures a parallel structural pattern: leaders integrated technology into core practice incrementally through low-risk, project-based learning, building mastery and institutional change without betting the firm on a single grand rollout [https://www.sloanreview.mit.edu/article/computeraided-architects-a-case-study-of-it-and-strategic-change/]. The transferable lesson is not "technology adoption." It is *sequenced redesign.*

The architect VP Sales installs:

- **Reference circuits** where experimentation is allowed and instrumented.
- **Release discipline** for play updates (versioned, segment-scoped, reversible).
- **Kill criteria** for initiatives that create activity without throughput.
- **Regime-based measurement** so averages don't hide failures.

The organization stops "rolling out change." It starts running controlled releases of execution behavior.

### 4) Cross-Functional Orchestration: Build One Company the Buyer Can Recognize

Cross-functional "alignment" is what organizations call it when they can't coordinate by design. In an agentic revenue system, alignment is too slow. You need orchestration: a shared execution fabric that makes coordination a runtime property.

Intelemark's cross-functional team guidance is blunt about the mechanics: break silos through shared vision, defined roles, regular operational check-ins, conflict management, and explicit inclusion of analysis capability (e.g., sales analysts) to improve decision-making and performance [https://www.intelemark.com/blog/cross-functional-teams-for-b2b-sales-success/]. That's not culture talk. That's coordination design.

Force Management's perspective reinforces the same system reality: improved execution comes when sales, customer success, and supporting functions operate with unified messaging, clear qualification standards, and coordinated workflows—because the customer journey is not owned by one function [https://www.forcemanagement.com/blog/selling-beyond-the-sales-team-how-a-cross-functional-approach-improves-execution].

The Product Marketing Alliance case offers a useful operational pattern: a leader built durable autonomy through cross-functional task forces, weekly alignments, "mission control" stand-ups, transparency, and shared processes during uncertainty—coordinating across regions and functions rather than relying on local improvisation [https://www.productmarketingalliance.com/leading-cross-functional-teams-in-a-global-organization/]. The mechanism matters: lightweight, high-frequency coordination that keeps execution coherent without endless negotiation.

The architect VP Sales becomes the orchestrator of:

- **Decision rights**: who governs what, and where the system is allowed to act.
- **Shared metrics**: latency, leakage, coverage, exception load, policy integrity.
- **Shared operating rhythms**: triage, loop health, play releases, autonomy boundary resets.
- **Cross-functional workflows** that suppress collisions before they reach the buyer.

The outcome is simple: the buyer experiences one company, not departmental interference patterns.

## The VP Sales Operating Model: Three Design Mandates

### Mandate 1: Replace "Deal Reviews" with "System Reviews"

Deal reviews are not management. They're salvage operations. They ask, "What happened here?"

System reviews ask, "What allowed this to happen repeatedly, and what mechanism prevents recurrence?"

This move forces the VP Sales to govern:

- signal-to-action latency,
- handoff integrity,
- exception routing quality,
- and the stability of definitions that agents execute against.

Deals still matter. But they become evidence of system health, not the system itself.

### Mandate 2: Make Autonomy Durable Through "Approved Lanes"

Autonomy fails when it is granted as freedom. It succeeds when it is granted as a lane: bounded authority with clear constraints and escalation.

In practice, durability comes from architecture:

- what the system can do without permission,
- what it must escalate,
- what it must never do,
- and how fast you can stop it when it drifts.

This is where experimentation, governance, and cross-functional orchestration converge into a single management discipline.

### Mandate 3: Convert Talent into IP

The heroic seller is expensive because their advantage is trapped inside them. The best organizations extract that advantage and encode it into repeatable system behavior.

Vivun's solution-architecture framing makes this explicit: centralized repositories, reusable solution patterns, and quantified business impact metrics turn seller expertise into institutional capability rather than individual wizardry [https://www.vivun.com/blog/solution-architecture-best-practices-for-sellers-from-design-to-revenue].

The architect VP Sales treats:

- top-performer behaviors as patterns to formalize,
- loss reasons as failure modes to engineer out,
- and playbooks as deployed behavior, not static documentation.

## Career Path Evolution: The Sales Leader Stops Being a Ladder Rung

The old career path rewarded scope: more accounts, bigger deals, more headcount, more meetings.

The new career path rewards system leverage: better loops, cleaner governance, higher throughput with lower noise.

This creates a new leadership archetype inside sales: people who can:

- design cross-functional circuits,
- use data to validate truth rather than argue it,
- run controlled experiments,

- and encode judgment into scalable mechanisms.

The MIT Sloan architecture case highlights the underlying career dynamic: mastery and professional identity evolved alongside embedded technology, built incrementally through project-based learning rather than abstract directives [https://www.sloanreview.mit.edu/article/computeraided-architects-a-case-study-of-it-and-strategic-change/]. Sales leadership will follow the same pattern: the next generation earns authority by shipping systems, not by shouting louder in forecast calls.

## Team Structure Evolution: From Pods of Sellers to Cells of Execution

Once execution becomes system-shaped, the "sales team" stops being a homogenous group of quota carriers. It becomes a set of specialized cells that govern different parts of the revenue machine.

Cross-functional models described in practice—clear roles, regular coordination, and explicit analytical support—point toward the shape: sales analysts and revenue operators embedded as first-class citizens in execution, not as report generators [https://www.intelemark.com/blog/cross-functional-teams-for-b2b-sales-success/].

The durable structure is not more layers. It is fewer handoffs and clearer ownership:

- **Field execution** (human trust and negotiation)
- **Revenue engineering** (workflow, routing, instrumentation)
- **Solution architecture** (reusable designs, edge-case testing)
- **Governance** (policies, constraints, approvals for irreversible moves)

This is how autonomy becomes durable: the system has owners, and those owners have mechanisms.

## Leadership Behavior Evolution: Calm Beats Charisma

The system architect VP Sales is not defined by intensity. They are defined by constraint design and loop integrity.

They stop performing urgency. They build the conditions where urgency is less necessary.

The APAC cross-functional leadership story is a reminder that orchestration is operational, not inspirational: mission-control stand-ups, shared processes, and persistent transparency produce resilience under uncertainty [https://www.productmarketingalliance.com/leading-cross-functional-teams-in-a-global-organization/]. That leadership style translates cleanly into agentic revenue: fewer speeches, more governed cadence.

The dry truth is this: if your revenue organization needs the VP Sales to be charismatic every week, the system is under-designed.

## The Inevitable Implication: VP Sales Becomes a Board-Level Systems Role

Boards will not evaluate the next decade of sales leadership primarily on "hitting the number." They will evaluate it on whether the company can produce revenue with lower volatility and higher throughput under complexity.

That is a systems question.

So the VP Sales either evolves into a system architect—systems thinking, data literacy, experimentation discipline, and cross-functional orchestration—or becomes the leader of a shrinking domain: human coordination in a world that has moved to governed autonomy.

The winners will not look frantic. They will look engineered.

Chapter 21

# Implementation Roadmap: From Vision to Working System

## The Transition Doesn't Fail in Strategy. It Fails in Sequence.

Most revenue leaders already have a "vision" for autonomy. What they don't have is a migration path that preserves revenue while redesigning the machine.

This is the executive trap: treating an operating system change like a feature rollout. You get pilots. You get dashboards. You get noise. You do not get a working system.

A 12–24 month roadmap is not a project plan. It is a controlled transfer of execution authority from humans into a governed architecture—lane by lane, loop by loop. That transfer has a sequence. You cannot skip it.

## The Roadmap at a Glance (12–24 Months)

The pattern repeats across successful transformations: assess reality, design the target, build foundations, ship a narrow circuit, scale with discipline, then institutionalize governance. Case studies from Walmart, AB InBev, and Sophos consistently reinforce staged planning and measurable progress tracking rather than big-bang change [https://disbug.io/en/blog/digital-transformation-case-studies-success-stories/] [https://amplitude.com/blog/digital-transformation-examples].

1. **Phase 0 (Weeks 0–4): Executive alignment + baseline assessment**
2. **Phase 1 (Months 1–3): Design principles + target operating model**
3. **Phase 2 (Months 3–6): Foundations (data, identity, event streams, controls)**
4. **Phase 3 (Months 6–9): First agentic "reference circuit" in production**
5. **Phase 4 (Months 9–15): Scaling patterns (repeatable lanes, cross-team rollout)**
6. **Phase 5 (Months 15–24): Governance as an institution (release cadence, audit, ROI, resilience)**

Your calendar may vary. The sequence does not.

## Phase 0 (Weeks 0–4): Baseline Assessment — Stop Guessing Where You Are

Transformation begins with a non-negotiable act: tell the truth about the current system. Not tool inventory. System behavior.

### What to assess (the only five questions that matter)

- **Truth count:** how many "official" pipeline and forecast numbers exist?
- **Workflow continuity:** where does work stall between functions?
- **Latency map:** where do signals wait for meetings to become action?
- **Exception load:** how often do humans arbitrate tool conflicts and handoffs?
- **Control readiness:** what actions are currently permitted, auditable, and reversible?

Walmart's transformation stories emphasize starting with current-state audits and customer/business pain points, then working forward from there rather than starting with technology [https://disbug.io/en/blog/digital-transformation-case-studies-success-stories/] [https://amplitude.com/blog/digital-transformation-examples]. Non-profit modernization roadmaps use the same discipline: document pain points, map current systems, then rationalize priorities before building [https://www.stgit.com/casestudy/digital-transformation-roadmap-definition-applications-modernizations/].

**Deliverable: The Revenue Reality Brief (10 pages, max)**

- One-page "current operating loop" diagram (signal → decision → action)
- Top 10 latency points (where time dies)
- Top 10 leakage points (where deals degrade quietly)
- Top 10 semantic conflicts (definitions that disagree across teams)
- Baseline metrics: cycle length by segment, stage conversion, coverage quality, forecast variance

If you cannot publish this brief without political edits, you are not ready for autonomy. You are still negotiating reality.

## Phase 1 (Months 1–3): Design Principles — The Constitution Before the Code

"Vision" is cheap. Design principles are enforceable. They tell the organization what it will *not* do.

### Non-negotiable design principles for an agentic revenue roadmap

- **One truth surface:** definitions are engineered, not debated.
- **Systems of action over systems of narration:** if it can't trigger governed behavior, it's secondary.
- **Approved lanes before broad autonomy:** authority expands only inside defined boundaries.
- **Exception packets, not alerts:** escalations must be contextual and actionable.
- **Release discipline:** plays and policies ship like product releases—versioned, measured, reversible.

AB InBev's transformation narratives repeatedly highlight setting vision/objectives and sequencing against a clear timeline, rather than attempting parallel modernization everywhere [https://disbug.io/en/blog/digital-transformation-case-studies-success-stories/] [https://amplitude.com/blog/digital-transformation-examples]. The RTI compendium reflects a similar structure: preparation and design precede action, then maintenance is governed as an operating discipline—not an afterthought [https://cdn.fs.pathlms.com/EUn5kdJvRwav7NNrdWyc?cache=true&dl=true].

**Deliverable: Target Operating Model (TOM) for Revenue Execution**

- Revenue loop definition (signal taxonomy, decision rights, action classes)
- Autonomy ladder target for 12 months and 24 months (what authority moves, what stays human)
- Named "reference circuit" selection (the first end-to-end workflow you will govern)
- Governance model: who owns policies, who owns orchestration integrity, who owns overrides

## Phase 2 (Months 3–6): Foundational Work — Build the Conditions Autonomy Requires

Every failed autonomy program shares one cause: it tried to act without stable truth and control surfaces. Foundations are not plumbing. Foundations are what allow you to delegate authority without embarrassment.

### Foundation A: Identity and system-of-record coherence

- Account and contact identity resolution (dedupe, match, merge)
- Canonical definitions for core states (account state, opportunity state, suppression state)
- Lineage: the system can explain where decision-driving fields came from

### Foundation B: Event streams (state change becomes executable)

- Define the revenue event taxonomy (what events matter, what is noise)
- Implement event capture for the reference circuit

- Set freshness SLAs (when an event arrives too late, it's operationally useless)

**Foundation C: Control architecture (permissioning, audit, rollback)**

- Action classes with permissions (send, suppress, route, update state, escalate)
- Audit trail requirements (who/what/when/why/policy version)
- Rollback mechanics (action override, play halt, lane kill switch)

AB InBev's staged path highlights foundational cloud/data work as a precursor to higher-order execution use cases [https://amplitude.com/blog/digital-transformation-examples]. STGIT's roadmap reinforces the same sequencing: foundational modernization (cloud/CRM/application work) before scaling, paired with governance through prioritized enhancements and disciplined delivery [https://www.stgit.com/casestudy/digital-transformation-roadmap-definition-applications-modernizations/].

### Deliverable: "Minimum Viable Truth for Action" (MVTA)

This is not "clean all the data." It is the smallest set of truth you will enforce because the system will act on it. If it isn't enforceable, it can't be foundational.

## Phase 3 (Months 6–9): Initial Agentic Use Cases — Ship One Reference Circuit

Your first agentic deployment should not be "AI in sales." It should be one end-to-end circuit where autonomy can be governed, measured, and improved.

### The reference circuit criteria

- **Cross-functional:** touches at least two teams (Sales + Marketing, or Sales + RevOps, etc.)
- **High-frequency:** runs daily, not quarterly
- **Reversible actions:** early autonomy should primarily be reversible to reduce blast radius
- **Clear outcome metric:** cycle compression, conversion lift, leakage reduction, or coverage quality improvement

**Two reference circuits that work in most organizations**

- **Inbound intent → routing → first response → meeting set** (latency and collision elimination)
- **Late-stage risk detection → suppression → escalation packet → intervention** (pipeline defense)

Sophos' transformation story emphasizes adoption enablement—training and metrics—because initial use cases only survive if operators can see the benefit and the organization can prove progress [https://disbug.io/en/blog/digital-transformation-case-studies-success-stories/]. Walmart/Ford examples similarly emphasize starting with specific applications/use cases, then expanding what works rather than declaring a universal rollout [https://amplitude.com/blog/digital-transformation-examples].

**Deliverable: Production pilot with "graduation gates"**

- Baseline vs. delta dashboard for the circuit (before/after)
- Exception packet standard (what escalations must include)

- Policy blocks and suppression logic live from day one
- Documented rollback drills completed (not planned)

## Phase 4 (Months 9–15): Scaling Patterns — Replicate Lanes, Not Experiments

Scaling is where most transformations commit their largest sin: copying activity instead of copying architecture. The goal is not "more use cases." The goal is repeatable lanes of governed autonomy.

### The scaling mechanism: cross-functional rollout by lane

- **Lane definition:** segment scope + allowed action classes + constraints + escalation triggers
- **Lane instrumentation:** latency, leakage, coverage, exception load, policy integrity
- **Lane expansion rule:** expand only when exception load decreases and outcomes improve simultaneously

AB InBev's supply chain digitization example illustrates scaling through disciplined rollout rather than isolated pilots—expanding a capability across the organization once proven [https://disbug.io/en/blog/digital-transformation-case-studies-success-stories/]. The RTI compendium similarly describes multi-stage journeys where "action" becomes sustainable only when maintenance and governance rhythms exist [https://cdn.fs.pathlms.com/EUn5kdJvRwav7NNrdWyc?cache=true&dl=true].

### The ADDEV Materials lesson: speed is useful when integration is real

ADDEV's case is instructive because it demonstrates a fast, ERP-integrated launch approach—initial value followed by expansion—without pretending the system can scale without foundations [https://oroinc.com/b2b-ecommerce/blog/case-studies-of-digital-transformation/].

### The Hershey lesson: scaling is where negligence becomes visible

Hershey's widely cited failure mode—rushed scaling and operational disruption—remains the simplest warning: you can modernize faster than the organization can absorb, and the bill arrives as customer impact [https://oroinc.com/b2b-ecommerce/blog/case-studies-of-digital-transformation/]. In agentic revenue, that "bill" looks like brand drift, duplicated outreach, forecast instability, and compliance panic.

### Deliverable: The Lane Library

- Lane definitions (approved lanes by segment and motion)
- Reusable suppression rules (collision avoidance as first-class logic)
- Release notes (versioned changes to plays and policy constraints)
- Decommission plan (what old workflows and tools are now obsolete)

## Phase 5 (Months 15–24): Governance — Make Autonomy a Managed Institution

By this point, the question is no longer "can it work?" The question is "can it stay sane?"

The most mature transformations treat governance as the system's metabolism: measurement, prioritization, and controlled evolution. Non-profit roadmap patterns emphasize governance as prioritized enhancements and measurable tracking to prevent drift—because drift is what quietly kills operating improvements [https://www.stgit.com/casestudy/digital-transformation-roadmap-definition-applications-modernizations/]. Walmart/AB InBev transformation stories similarly reinforce milestone planning, risk mitigation, and ongoing measurement as the price of durable change [https://disbug.io/en/blog/digital-transformation-case-studies-success-stories/].

### The governance operating cadence (the minimum viable rhythm)

- **Daily:** exception triage (what escalated, what was suppressed, what needs human judgment)
- **Weekly:** loop health review (latency, leakage, coverage, exception load, policy blocks)
- **Monthly:** release governance (plays/policies versioned, measured, reversible)
- **Quarterly:** autonomy boundary reset (expand/tighten lanes based on evidence)

### Deliverable: The Autonomy Board Pack

- Throughput: cycle length, conversion, velocity (by segment)
- Coverage: % book receiving baseline "good execution"

- Control: policy blocks, rollback events, incident time-to-contain
- Economics: ROI by lane, payback status, cost to run governance

If you cannot report these without a war room, you did not build governed autonomy. You built automated motion and called it progress.

## The 12–24 Month Roadmap Checklist (CEO / CRO / Board Version)

### Assessment (Weeks 0–4)

- We have a published current-state Revenue Reality Brief.
- We can state truth count for pipeline and forecast (and it is trending toward 1).
- We have a quantified latency map and leakage map.

### Design (Months 1–3)

- We have explicit design principles that constrain what we will and won't automate.
- We have selected one cross-functional reference circuit.

- Decision rights are written: what the system decides, what humans decide, what is conditional.

**Foundations (Months 3–6)**

- Identity integrity exists for accounts/contacts used in the reference circuit.
- Canonical states are enforced for the reference circuit.
- Event stream is live for the reference circuit with freshness SLAs.
- Permissions, auditability, and rollback exist before broad action is enabled.

**Initial use cases (Months 6–9)**

- Reference circuit is in production with baseline vs. delta metrics.
- Exceptions are packaged (not alerts).
- Suppression rules prevent collisions and fatigue by design.

**Scaling (Months 9–15)**

- We scale by lane (approved lanes), not by scattered pilots.
- Lane Library exists and is versioned.

- We actively decommission obsolete workflows and reduce parallel automation.

### Governance (Months 15–24)

- We have a release cadence for plays/policies with measurement and rollback discipline.
- We can show ROI by lane and payback timelines without hand-waving.
- Autonomy boundaries expand only when control and outcomes improve together.

## The Inevitable Implication: You Will Either Migrate to a Governable System—or You Will Run a Faster Mess

The market is not waiting for your organization chart to feel aligned. It is rewarding firms that convert intent into execution faster, with fewer collisions and less drift.

That advantage does not come from adopting tools. It comes from shipping a system—sequenced, governed, measured—until autonomy becomes a stable operating capability.

The roadmap is not optional. It is the cost of remaining credible while you redesign how revenue is produced.

Chapter 22

# Case Patterns: How Different Models Go Agentic

## The Pattern Is Not "Agents." It's Where Authority Moves.

Most "case studies" are written like marketing. They list features and show charts. They miss the only question that matters:

**Where did execution authority move—from humans into the system—and what became structurally possible as a result?**

Agentic systems do not create advantage by being clever. They create advantage by changing the operating model:

- From queued work to event-driven work.
- From manual triage to autonomous routing.
- From dashboards to interventions.
- From approval chains to bounded autonomy.

This chapter is not a gallery of success stories. It is a set of archetypes. You will recognize your business in one of them. Then you will see what, specifically, has to be redesigned.

## The Three Archetypes (And Why They Behave Differently)

Most go-to-market systems fall into three operating conditions:

- **Mid-market SaaS**: high volume of interactions, thin teams, customer communication happens in messy, human channels.
- **Complex enterprise**: multi-stakeholder buying, slow approvals, many systems, high coordination drag.
- **Usage-based models**: revenue is downstream of adoption and retention, not just closed-won.

All three can go agentic. But they go agentic through different choke points.

## What Travels Across Contexts (The Portable Architecture)

Before the specifics, name the elements that travel. These are not "best practices." They are repeatable structural moves.

### 1) Event-Driven Execution

Agents that wait for forms or tickets are still working on human cadence. The durable pattern is event-driven: state changes trigger action continuously. That architecture is explicitly described as a core trait of high-performing agent systems—agents triggered by real-time events rather than batched workflows [https://www.invimatic.com/blog/the-architecture-behind-high-performing-ai-agents-in-modern-saas-products/].

### 2) Planning Decomposition

The highest-leverage agents do not "do a task." They decompose a workflow into phases, confirm completion at each phase, then select the next move. That pattern shows up starkly in security response automation where workflows are partitioned into intake, assessment, execution, escalation [https://azure.microsoft.com/en-us/blog/agent-factory-the-new-era-of-agentic-ai-common-use-cases-and-design-patterns/].

### 3) Human-in-the-Loop as a Routing System, Not an Approval Ritual

HITL that requires manual approval for everything is a new bottleneck. HITL that routes only uncertainty to humans is a control surface. Across modern agent design, the recurring mechanism is: let the system run the fast loop, escalate exceptions with context [https://www.invimatic.com/blog/the-architecture-behind-high-performing-ai-agents-in-modern-saas-products/].

### 4) "Value Pricing" Emerges When Work is Actually Removed

When agents don't just assist but execute end-to-end, vendors and internal teams can price, measure, and govern against value delivered rather than usage. That shift is explicitly called out as agentic systems remove human hours and backlogs—making value-based economics viable [https://www.cathaycapital.com/agentic-ai-is-a-massive-opportunity-for-b2b-software/].

Those are the portable components. Now the important part: where each model must tailor, and where leaders often create friction by importing the wrong assumptions.

## Archetype 1: Mid-Market SaaS — "Execution Happens Where Customers Already Are"

Mid-market SaaS fails in coordination, not strategy. The signal is abundant. The team is thin. The operating model breaks at the interface between customer communication and internal triage.

### The Hightouch Pattern: Stop Forcing Customers Into Your Workflow

Hightouch faced an operational reality: 300+ shared customer Slack channels created impossible manual triage. The normal enterprise response would be to force a ticketing model onto customers. They did the opposite. They pushed execution into Slack itself—deploying agents in-channel to prompt self-service resolution [https://www.usepylon.com/blog/agentic-ai-use-cases].

Reported outcomes are not subtle: 75% increase in self-service and 100 hours saved per month for the support team [https://www.usepylon.com/blog/agentic-ai-use-cases].

### Why This Created Outsized Leverage

This wasn't "better support." It was operating model inversion:

- **Old model:** customer asks in Slack → humans translate into internal systems → humans decide → humans respond.
- **Agentic model:** customer asks in Slack → system classifies, retrieves, proposes/executes resolution → humans handle exceptions.

The leverage is not the hours saved. It's that response-time and coverage stop being constrained by the number of humans watching channels. You are no longer staffing attention. You are staffing exceptions.

### The Tailoring Requirement: Channel is Architecture

The detail most leaders misread is the integration point. Slack wasn't a "nice-to-have." It was the primary execution surface for that customer base. Mid-market SaaS organizations that treat Slack as secondary will build agents in the wrong place, then complain adoption is low.

Event-driven agents working inside the customer's native channel is a common design pattern for modern agentic systems [https://www.invimatic.com/blog/the-architecture-behind-high-performing-ai-agents-in-modern-saas-products/]. The channel choice is not UX. It's where the loop closes.

### The Friction Trap: Automating the Back Office While the Front Office Stays Manual

Mid-market SaaS leaders often automate internal workflows first because it feels safer. Then they discover the real bottleneck remained: customer interaction still requires human routing and context assembly. They improved the machine room and left the front door staffed by heroics.

## Archetype 2: Complex Enterprise — "Autonomy Wins in the White Space Between Systems"

Enterprise revenue environments do not suffer from a lack of tools. They suffer from cross-system execution debt: approvals, policy enforcement, routing, and identity across platforms. The constraint is not intelligence. The constraint is orchestration under governance.

### The Invoice-to-Approval Pattern: Intent Interpretation + Cross-System Execution

A global financial services company implemented agentic AI to connect core enterprise systems and execute end-to-end finance workflows: extracting invoice details, matching purchase orders, and generating expense reports automatically [https://www.moveworks.com/us/en/resources/blog/agentic-ai-examples-use-cases].

This matters because it shows the enterprise version of autonomy. It's not about "doing tasks faster." It's about eliminating multi-system queueing as an operating condition.

### Why This Is an Enterprise Blueprint (Not a Finance Story)

Enterprise revenue has the same pathology as enterprise finance:

- Requests arrive in human language, not in clean form fields.
- Execution requires multiple systems with different permissions.
- Approvals create bottlenecks that become normalized.

- People become the integration layer.

The agentic leap is end-to-end action under policy—so the backlog shrinks because it stops being created.

### The Second-Order Effect: Economics Shift Toward Value Delivered

When the system executes full loops, the economic model can move away from usage and toward value delivered—hours removed from workflows, backlogs eliminated, throughput restored [https://www.cathaycapital.com/agentic-ai-is-a-massive-opportunity-for-b2b-software/].

This is larger than pricing. It changes how the enterprise funds capability: from "software as cost center" to "execution as a measurable value stream."

### The Tailoring Requirement: Policy Enforcement Is Not Optional

The enterprise does not merely need an agent that can act. It needs an agent that can act *only* inside permissioned boundaries—secure access control, policy enforcement, audit trails. The cases that scale in regulated environments treat this as table stakes, not a later enhancement [https://www.moveworks.com/us/en/resources/blog/agentic-ai-examples-use-cases].

### The Friction Trap: Enterprise Autonomy Without Identity Coherence

Enterprise architectures break when "the same thing" is not the same thing across systems. If vendor identity, contract objects, approval corridors, or stakeholder roles are inconsistent, agents don't just make errors. They execute contradictions. Fast.

## Archetype 3: Complex Enterprise Sales — "Routing Is the Revenue Control System"

Enterprise sales leaders spend months talking about messaging and enablement. Then they quietly lose deals to something less poetic: response time, routing accuracy, and stakeholder fit.

### Lead Qualification + Routing at Scale: How Latency Becomes a Loss Mechanism

Agentic systems are now being used to automate lead qualification by analyzing customer data, behavioral patterns, website analytics, email engagement, and demographics—then routing qualified prospects immediately [https://kodexolabs.com/agentic-ai-use-cases/].

Reported results include lead conversion improvements of up to 40% in teams that eliminate response-time friction through agentic qualification and routing [https://kodexolabs.com/agentic-ai-use-cases/].

### Why Routing Creates Outsized Leverage

Routing is not administration. Routing is how you allocate the scarcest asset in enterprise sales: high-trust human time.

When routing is late or wrong:

- The buyer experiences indifference.
- The conversation begins with mismatched context.
- The deal starts with hidden friction.

Agentic routing changes the physics: signal → qualification → assignment → engagement becomes a continuous loop, not a weekly hygiene ritual.

### The Tailoring Requirement: Enterprise Is a Buying-Group Problem, Not a Lead Problem

This is where generic automation fails. Enterprise deals are not “leads.” They are stakeholder networks.

Routing logic must incorporate account context and multi-stakeholder realities, not just form fills and clicks. That is why enterprise deployments require customized scoring and routing logic rather than generic "hot lead" models [https://kodexolabs.com/agentic-ai-use-cases/].

### The Friction Trap: Over-Confidence in Scores Becomes False Certainty

A routing engine that looks precise can create the worst kind of executive error: false confidence. Leaders stop asking whether the system is correct and start expanding volume—until pipeline quality degrades quietly. In enterprise sales, misrouted attention is not a small inefficiency. It's strategic waste.

## Archetype 4: Usage-Based Models — "Retention is Not a Team. It's a Sensor Network."

Usage-based businesses don't primarily lose revenue at the sales stage. They lose revenue through silent decay: adoption stalls, value realization slips, churn risk crystallizes before anyone intervenes.

### The Proactive Customer Success Monitoring Pattern

Agentic systems monitor usage patterns continuously and trigger proactive intervention when churn signals or unmet needs appear—rather than waiting for customers to report problems [https://www.getmonetizely.com/articles/28-realistic-agentic-ai-use-cases-that-could-transform-horizontal-saas-categories].

### Why This Is Structurally Different From Seat-Based SaaS

Usage-based models have a brutal truth:

**Your revenue is a live function of customer behavior.**

That means customer success is not a "function." It is the operating layer that defends revenue integrity. Proactive monitoring is not a nice improvement. It is revenue architecture.

### The Tailoring Requirement: Intervention Timing Must Be Governed, Not Opportunistic

In usage-based systems, it's easy to overreach: nudges become noise, outreach becomes fatigue, "help" becomes interruption. The system must be able to suppress as well as trigger. Without suppression design, proactive monitoring becomes proactive annoyance.

### The Friction Trap: Measuring the Wrong Outcome

Usage-based companies often evaluate CS automation on "tickets reduced" or "tasks automated." That misses the unit economics. The correct outcomes are:

- retention stability,
- time-to-value compression,
- expansion capture inside high-health states.

When you measure wrong, you optimize wrong—and then conclude "agents didn't help." They did what you asked. You asked poorly.

## Archetype 5: Mid-Market Security Ops — "Planning Agents Create a New Cost Curve"

Security operations is often dismissed as "not revenue." That's the wrong lens. Security ops is a high-frequency, high-stakes execution environment with scarce expert labor—exactly the environment where agentic architecture reveals what it can really do.

### ContraForce: Planning Agents That Phase-Check Work

ContraForce's Agentic Security Delivery Platform decomposes incident response into phases—intake, impact assessment, playbook execution, escalation—

checking for next steps after each phase [https://azure.microsoft.com/en-us/blog/agent-factory-the-new-era-of-agentic-ai-common-use-cases-and-design-patterns/].

Reported outcomes: 80% of incident investigation and response automated, with full investigation processed for less than $1 per incident [https://azure.microsoft.com/en-us/blog/agent-factory-the-new-era-of-agentic-ai-common-use-cases-and-design-patterns/].

### The Structural Lesson for Revenue Leaders

The relevant transfer is not the domain. It's the control design:

- Break complex workflows into governable phases.
- Require completion checks before progression.
- Escalate only when evidence is incomplete or risk rises.

That is exactly how revenue should treat late-stage deal management: intake (signal), assessment (risk drivers), play execution (interventions), escalation (human judgment).

### The Tailoring Requirement: Auditability is the Product

In security, "it worked" is not enough. Evidence, explainability, and audit trails are the work. Security requires custom patterns around evidence collection and compliance documentation because general-purpose agents lack the necessary forensic integrity [https://azure.microsoft.com/en-us/blog/agent-factory-the-new-era-of-agentic-ai-common-use-cases-and-design-patterns/].

Revenue has its own equivalent: pricing exceptions, claims compliance, and customer-facing commitments. When autonomy touches those, auditability becomes non-negotiable.

## The Cross-Case Distinction: What Created Leverage vs. What Created Friction

### Leverage Came From Three Decisions

- **They moved execution into the native workflow surface.** Hightouch didn't build an agent "for support." They built it where support actually happens: Slack [https://www.usepylon.com/blog/agentic-ai-use-cases].

- **They targeted high-frequency, high-friction loops first.** Invoice-to-approval backlogs, lead routing delays, incident response phases—these are compounding loops. Fixing them compounds [https://www.moveworks.com/us/en/resources/blog/agentic-ai-examples-use-cases] [https://kodexolabs.com/agentic-ai-use-cases/] [https://azure.microsoft.com/en-us/blog/agent-factory-the-new-era-of-agentic-ai-common-use-cases-and-design-patterns/].
- **They treated HITL as exception governance, not blanket approvals.** Modern agent performance patterns rely on bounded autonomy and human escalation at uncertainty boundaries—not humans approving every move [https://www.invimatic.com/blog/the-architecture-behind-high-performing-ai-agents-in-modern-saas-products/].

### Friction Came From Three Predictable Mistakes

- **Building agents beside workflows instead of inside them.** Optional "AI assistants" don't redesign execution. They decorate it.

- **Importing generic models into contexts that require tailored semantics.** Enterprise sales routing fails when it ignores buying-group complexity and account context [https://kodexolabs.com/agentic-ai-use-cases/].
- **Underestimating governance as an enabling constraint.** Regulated environments require secure access control and policy enforcement to scale autonomy without incidents [https://www.moveworks.com/us/en/resources/blog/agentic-ai-examples-use-cases]. Without it, autonomy is not fast. It is reckless.

## The Executive Model: "Travel Kit" vs. "Tailoring Kit"

If you want your organization to move quickly without repeating other people's mistakes, use two kits.

### The Travel Kit (Always the Same)

- Event-driven triggers that collapse latency [https://www.invimatic.com/blog/the-architecture-behind-high-performing-ai-agents-in-modern-saas-products/]

- Planning decomposition into phases with completion checks [https://azure.microsoft.com/en-us/blog/agent-factory-the-new-era-of-agentic-ai-common-use-cases-and-design-patterns/]
- Exception-based HITL supervision [https://www.invimatic.com/blog/the-architecture-behind-high-performing-ai-agents-in-modern-saas-products/]
- Value measurement tied to work removed, not activity added [https://www.cathaycapital.com/agentic-ai-is-a-massive-opportunity-for-b2b-software/]

### The Tailoring Kit (Always Specific)

- **Workflow surface:** Slack-first vs. ticket-first vs. CRM-first [https://www.usepylon.com/blog/agentic-ai-use-cases]
- **Semantic objects:** lead vs. buying group vs. account state [https://kodexolabs.com/agentic-ai-use-cases/]
- **Governance intensity:** auditability and policy enforcement by risk class

[https://www.moveworks.com/us/en/resources/blog/agentic-ai-examples-use-cases]

- **Economic objective:** churn prevention and adoption stability in usage-based models [https://www.getmonetizely.com/articles/28-realistic-agentic-ai-use-cases-that-could-transform-horizontal-saas-categories]

## The Inevitable Implication: The Next Advantage Is Not "Adoption." It's Architecture Fit.

Over the next cycle, most companies will attempt to replicate outcomes by copying tools. They will be confused when it doesn't work.

Because what produced leverage in these patterns wasn't the agent. It was fit between:

- the business model,
- the execution loop,
- the workflow surface,
- and the governance constraint.

Mid-market SaaS wins when it embeds autonomy where customers already live. Enterprise wins when it converts cross-system friction into governed execution.

Usage-based models win when retention becomes an always-on sensing and intervention loop.

Treating every context the same produces the same result: expensive motion and very little control.

Agentic advantage will accrue to leaders who can do one thing consistently:

**move authority into the system without losing the right to govern it.**

Chapter 23

# Leading Through the Friction

## The Friction Is Not a Bug. It's the Evidence.

Revenue re-architecture is not a change program. It is a redistribution of authority.

You are moving execution power out of individual discretion and into a governed system. That transfer will create resistance even when the strategy is correct. Not because your people are irrational. Because the old operating model gave them status, cover, and control.

Most leaders misread this moment. They treat friction as a communications problem. It isn't. It's a structural transition showing up as politics, emotion, and temporary throughput loss.

The goal of this chapter is simple: lead the transition without letting the organization talk you out of the redesign.

## The Three Predictable Sources of Friction

### 1) Political Friction: You Are Taking Away Private Advantage

In the old model, power lived in what only certain people knew: which deals were real, which contacts mattered, which exceptions were possible, which internal shortcuts existed.

An agentic revenue system makes that private advantage legible. It exposes hidden work, silent deal decay, and ungoverned exceptions. That is why the loudest opposition often comes from the people who look the most "experienced."

They are not defending the company. They are defending their position inside the old system.

### 2) Organizational Friction: The Org Chart Was Built for Negotiation, Not Execution

Revenue functions were designed to bargain with each other: lead quality, attribution, pipeline definitions, forecast narratives, discount exceptions. Meetings were the arbitration layer.

Agentic execution reduces the space for negotiation. The system needs declared rules, not recurring debate. So the organization experiences the transition as loss of flexibility—when it is actually loss of ambiguity.

### 3) Emotional Friction: The Identity of "Greatness" Changes

Heroic selling rewarded endurance and improvisation. The agentic model rewards judgment, governance, and escalation quality.

That shift is not neutral. It changes who gets praised, promoted, and trusted. If you don't name that explicitly, the organization will interpret the redesign as a quiet demotion.

## The First Rule: Start With the Real Problem, Not the Solution

Most transformations stall because leadership cannot state the underlying strategic problem in one sentence. So they substitute a solution: "We're modernizing revenue," "We're implementing AI," "We're improving forecasting."

That creates immediate resistance because the organization doesn't know what pain you're solving—only what disruption you're imposing.

Harvard Business School research is blunt on the sequencing: restructuring is more likely to succeed when managers first understand the fundamental business problem they face [https://www.library.hbs.edu/working-knowledge/how-to-make-restructuring-work-for-your-company].

In agentic revenue terms, your "why" is usually one of these structural failures:

- Execution latency is now a competitive disadvantage, not an inconvenience.
- Truth is negotiated across functions, so the company cannot act without meetings.
- Revenue reliability depends on heroics, so scale increases volatility.
- Tooling increased output, but not control—so complexity is compounding.

Pick the real one. State it cleanly. Repeat it until it becomes operational reality, not leadership flavor.

## Boards Don't Fear Change. They Fear Unbounded Change.

Board friction is rarely ideological. It's structural.

Boards fund predictability. Re-architecting revenue threatens predictability in the short term—even when it creates it in the long term.

The mistake is treating the board like a checkpoint: notify them, then proceed. That is how you trigger late-stage skepticism when the first dip hits.

If you want transformation to survive, the board must be engaged as an operating partner, not a distant reviewer. Board guidance on successful transformation emphasizes that hands-on board involvement reduces risk and keeps initiatives on track, with transparent communication as a central discipline [https://boardmember.com/successful-transformation-demands-a-hands-on-board/].

### The Board Contract: Three Things You Must Promise

- **Bounded authority:** autonomy expands only inside declared lanes, with explicit decision rights.
- **Measurable progression:** the board will see leading indicators, not just quarter-end outcomes.
- **Reversibility:** there is a real rollback posture when policies or plays misfire.

### The Board Pack That Prevents Panic

Do not over-index on "AI progress." Boards don't buy intelligence. They buy control. Bring a pack that makes control legible:

- **Truth count:** how many "official" pipeline/forecast numbers exist (trend to one).
- **Latency:** signal-to-action time in the reference circuit.
- **Leakage:** stalled-state duration and silent deal death rates.
- **Exception load:** escalations per 100 opportunities, with time-to-resolution.
- **Risk posture:** policy blocks, suppression triggers, rollback events.

This changes the board conversation from "Is this risky?" to "Is this governed?" That is the only conversation in which autonomy gets funded through a dip.

## Redirecting Skeptics: Stop Debating Opinions. Install Calibration.

Skeptics in revenue transformations are rarely wrong about the past. They are wrong about what the future will punish.

The fastest way to neutralize skepticism is not persuasion. It is calibration: make forecasts and operating claims verifiably accurate, repeatedly, until disbelief becomes expensive to maintain.

One practical executive reporting standard is simple: when forecasts consistently land within ~5% variance, the conversation shifts from "can we trust the numbers?" to "how do we accelerate growth?" [https://www.flowguide.io/post/board-ready-forecasts-growth-plans-the-sales-leader-s-guide-to-executive-reporting-excellence].

### Use "Verification, Not Confidence" as the New Language

In the old system, leaders asked reps, "How confident are you?" In the new system, leaders ask, "What evidence would change our probability?"

That single language shift does two things:

- It removes ego from forecasting.
- It forces the organization to improve signal integrity rather than polish narratives.

### The Skeptic's Trap You Must Avoid

You will be tempted to win the argument with a better deck. Don't.

Skeptics don't need storytelling. They need repeatability. So you don't "sell" them autonomy. You run a reference circuit, publish baseline vs. delta, and let arithmetic do what charisma cannot.

## The Productivity Dip: Why It Happens, and Why It's Not a Failure

There will be a dip. If there isn't, you probably didn't change anything that mattered.

The dip is caused by three mechanisms:

- **Process unlearning:** people lose their old shortcuts before the new system becomes muscle memory.
- **Governance installation:** constraints feel slower than improvisation—until they eliminate rework and collisions.

- **Role repositioning:** humans stop doing routine orchestration but haven't yet moved cleanly into exception judgment and trust work.

The executive mistake is treating the dip as proof the redesign is wrong. It's usually proof the redesign is real.

### Do Not Fund the Dip by Cutting the Future

When productivity drops, finance reflexes activate: "reduce cost," "pause investment," "freeze headcount," "cut programs."

Sometimes that is necessary. Often it is self-sabotage: you cut the very capabilities required to exit the dip.

CFO restructuring guidance emphasizes the balancing act: cost rationalization must avoid cuts that hinder key operations or stifle growth investment, requiring deliberate pacing rather than indiscriminate reduction [https://level10cfo.com/insights-into-effective-business-restructuring-from-a-cfo-s-perspective/].

In agentic revenue, the wrong cuts are predictable:

- RevOps capacity (you will need control engineering, not less of it).
- Data governance and integration work (without it, autonomy becomes noise).

- Enablement focused on new decision rights and escalation behavior (not generic training).

Cut those and you don't "stabilize." You extend the dip and call it prudence.

## When to Push vs. When to Stabilize: The Executive Pacing Model

Most leaders run transformations on mood: push when momentum feels good, pause when resistance gets loud. That is not leadership. That is responsiveness.

You need pacing rules that make the right action inevitable.

### Push When These Three Conditions Are True

- **Control surfaces exist:** permissions, auditability, rollback are real, not planned.
- **Exception load is trending down:** the system is getting quieter while throughput improves.
- **Baseline execution is improving:** coverage and loop closure increase without heroics.

### Stabilize When Any Two of These Appear

- **Truth divergence rises:** more than one "official" number starts circulating again.

- **Exception quality drops:** escalations become alerts instead of packets with options.
- **Shadow workflows proliferate:** Slack-based routing, spreadsheets, off-system approvals return.
- **Policy anxiety spikes:** people slow execution because they don't know what is allowed.

Stabilization is not retreat. It is tightening the machine before you increase speed.

## Communication That Works: Replace Reassurance With Precision

In transformations, leaders often try to calm people by being vague: "Everything will be fine," "This will make us faster," "Trust the process."

Vagueness creates fear because it signals a lack of control.

The communication discipline is simple:

- **Name what changes.** "Decision rights are moving into the system in these lanes."

- **Name what stays human.** "Pricing exceptions, commitments, and account strategy pivots remain human."
- **Name what will be measured.** "Latency, leakage, exception load, and rollback time-to-contain."
- **Name the sequence.** "One reference circuit, then lanes, then scale."

McKinsey research on growth transformers highlights a behavioral pattern leaders should steal: start from competitive insights and execute simultaneous initiatives at scale, anchored in quantified opportunity, to reduce uncertainty and sustain momentum [https://www.mckinsey.com/capabilities/transformation/our-insights/breaking-the-mold-five-behaviors-of-leading-growth-transformers].

The transferable point is not "do more at once." It is: communicate the plan as a set of measurable movements tied to external reality, not internal aspiration. When the story is grounded in competitive physics, fewer people treat it as optional.

## The Internal Politics You Must Preempt

### Politics Pattern #1: "This Is an Ops Project"

If the organization believes autonomy is a RevOps or tooling initiative, it will fail. Because it requires cross-functional authority redesign. Make it explicit: this is an operating system migration. It belongs to the CEO/CRO axis, with RevOps as control engineering.

### Politics Pattern #2: "Compliance Is Slowing Us Down"

Un-governed autonomy creates incidents. Incidents create freezes. Freezes create shadow execution. The fastest organizations do not bypass constraints. They encode constraints so they can move at speed inside safe lanes.

### Politics Pattern #3: "We Tried This Before"

Most companies did try something before. They tried tooling without architecture. Acknowledge it. Then draw the distinction: this time, governance and production lanes are part of the design from day one.

## The Leadership Posture: Calm, Clinical, Unmoved by Theater

This transition will produce noise. Some of it will be real signals. Much of it will be organizational bargaining.

Your job is not to win every conversation. Your job is to keep the redesign moving while protecting revenue continuity. That demands a posture that is:

- **Calm** enough to prevent panic behaviors.
- **Clinical** enough to focus on mechanism, not blame.
- **Firm** enough to not renegotiate the redesign every time the quarter tightens.

## The Inevitable Implication: Friction Is the Toll for Structural Advantage

You cannot re-architect revenue without surfacing the politics that the old system hid, the inconsistencies that meetings papered over, and the identity shifts that hero culture rewarded.

The leaders who win this era will not be the ones who "manage change" best. They will be the ones who can:

- engage the board as an operating partner [https://boardmember.com/successful-transformation-demands-a-hands-on-board/],
- neutralize skepticism through forecasting calibration and verified deltas [https://www.flowguide.io/post/board-ready-forecasts-growth-plans-the-sales-leader-s-guide-to-executive-reporting-excellence],
- pace investment without cutting the capabilities required to exit the dip [https://level10cfo.com/insights-into-effective-business-restructuring-from-a-cfo-s-perspective/],
- and anchor the organization in the real strategic problem so resistance has nowhere to hide [https://www.library.hbs.edu/working-knowledge/how-to-make-restructuring-work-for-your-company].

Friction is not a reason to stop. It is the confirmation that authority is actually moving. And authority is where competitive advantage now lives.

Chapter 24

# The Next Decade of Commercial Advantage

## The Next Competitive Moat Won't Be Strategy. It Will Be Execution Physics.

For the last three decades, commercial advantage was explained with familiar language: positioning, product, brand, distribution, talent. Those still matter. But they are no longer the decisive constraint.

The constraint is now execution throughput under complexity. Not "can we decide?" Can we *carry* the decision into the market, across functions, with speed, consistency, and control.

That is what agentic systems change. Not because intelligence is new. Because *autonomous execution* is becoming a core organizational capability.

The next decade will separate companies into two categories:

- Those that treat autonomy as a feature layer on top of the old operating model.
- Those that treat autonomy as the operating model—and redesign accordingly.

The first group will accumulate tools. The second group will accumulate structural advantage.

## The Structural Shift: Every Company Becomes a Two-Workforce Organization

In the old model, the workforce was human. Technology supported it. In the new model, the workforce becomes dual:

- **Human workforce**: judgment, trust, negotiation, exception handling, accountability.
- **Autonomous workforce**: continuous monitoring, orchestration, execution, and loop closure inside governed lanes.

This is not headcount reduction as ideology. It is a redesign of what "capacity" means.

The most misunderstood implication is also the most important: autonomous capacity is not distributed evenly across companies. It compounds where architecture exists to contain it. It stalls where governance, data, and workflows remain disputed.

Deloitte notes that 42% of firms are developing agentic roadmaps—explicitly emphasizing operating model redesign and ROI discipline over "automation layering," with domain pilots and partnerships improving deployment success [https://www.deloitte.com/us/en/insights/topics/technology-management/tech-trends/2026/agentic-ai-strategy.html]. That is not a trend line. It is the early shape of a new baseline.

## How GTM Strategy Changes When Execution Is Always-On

Most GTM strategy was designed for a simple truth: execution is scarce. So strategy focused on where to deploy humans: which segments, which channels, which plays. When execution becomes continuous, strategy changes form. It becomes constraint design.

### Shift 1: From Campaigns to Control Loops

In a human-timed organization, GTM is episodic. Plan, launch, measure, revise. In an autonomous organization, GTM becomes a set of always-on loops: detect → decide → act → learn.

This is why "more AI tools" disappoint. They don't create loops. They create commentary. Autonomous execution creates loops because it carries action across systems without waiting for meetings.

### Shift 2: From Volume Advantage to Latency Advantage

When the system can execute continuously, the competitive unit stops being "activity." It becomes *response time with coherence.*

This doesn't just change marketing and outbound. It changes the entire customer lifecycle:

- Intent is detected sooner.
- Follow-through happens reliably.
- Risks are surfaced before they harden.
- Expansion is triggered by evidence, not calendar.

Most companies will keep debating narratives in weekly cadences. Agentic competitors will operate in event-time. That gap becomes structural.

## Organizational Design: The Company Stops Scaling by Adding People

The loudest misunderstanding executives carry into this decade is that agentic systems are a productivity layer. They are not. They are a redefinition of organizational shape.

When autonomous execution becomes real, three things happen inside the org chart:

- **Execution moves into the system** (routine motion becomes machine-speed and governed).
- **Humans move upward** (from coordination to judgment and exception work).
- **Management becomes control engineering** (from inspection to policy, lanes, audit, and rollback).

### What the "Autonomous Operating Model" Looks Like in the Wild

Stonehill Innovation describes organizations embedding AI into engineering and finance workflows—proposal generation acceleration in firms like AECOM/Jacobs, and exception-driven finance automation in Siemens/IBM—paired with results-based monitoring, replication across units, and repositioning humans toward oversight [https://www.stonehillinnovation.com/blog/c4xjt3i83mm08w2fii1kkgsd9emces]. Read that as operating model economics:

- Cycle time compresses because work no longer waits for availability.

- Consistency rises because workflows become enforceable.
- Headcount leverage appears because supervision scales faster than execution labor.

The enduring advantage is not “doing the same work cheaper.” It is unlocking a new growth curve where throughput is no longer gated by hiring velocity.

### The 4-Phase Deployment Pattern Is the Real Competitive IP

A mid-sized manufacturer’s 4-phase agentic deployment—autonomous supply chain monitoring, vendor negotiation, inventory optimization, and customer service agents handling multi-step interactions—produced a 42% stockout reduction, 28% lower costs, and 65% faster response times, with pilots, metrics, and scaling discipline framed as foundations (data governance and change management) [https://agentic-ai-solutions.com/blog/agentic-ai-examples-business-transformation-2026/].

That story matters because it exposes what leaders miss: the advantage did not come from an isolated “agent.” It came from *institutionalizing* deployment sequencing and governance so autonomy could expand safely.

The companies that win will not have better tool selection. They will have better autonomy deployment mechanics. That becomes replicable advantage across every commercial workflow.

## M&A Will Be Repriced Around Integration Speed, Not Synergy Stories

M&A has always been sold with synergy math. In practice, value is captured—or lost—through integration throughput. Autonomous execution changes that throughput.

In the next decade, acquirers will quietly separate into two types:

- **Tool-portfolio acquirers**: add assets, then spend years stitching systems, roles, and workflows.
- **Execution-platform acquirers**: integrate faster because execution is already engineered as a governed fabric.

This is not a finance nuance. It decides whether you can compound acquisitions or merely accumulate them.

## Why Autonomous Process Automation Is an M&A Capability

KeyBank's enterprise automation scale—automating 300 processes across transactions, compliance, and service—reflects a shift toward end-to-end workflow execution across siloed systems, improving efficiency, reducing errors, and supporting compliance [https://www.automationanywhere.com/rpa/autonomous-enterprise].

The commercial translation is direct: an enterprise that can standardize and govern cross-system execution can integrate acquisitions faster because:

- Process becomes portable.
- Controls become enforceable.
- Exceptions become routable.
- Operational truth becomes alignable at runtime.

M&A due diligence will increasingly ask a new question:

**Can this company absorb another operating model without breaking execution?**

Autonomous execution is how that becomes "yes" by design, not by heroics.

## Backlogs Are the Signature of a Non-Agentic Operating Model

Moveworks describes a financial services firm deploying multi-agent finance operations to match invoices, process expense reports, and manage approvals across systems—eliminating backlogs through reasoning, planning, tool execution, and adaptation [https://www.moveworks.com/us/en/resources/blog/agentic-ai-examples-use-cases].

Backlog elimination is the tell. Backlogs aren't "too much work." Backlogs are a structural symptom of human-gated coordination across systems.

In M&A, backlog physics matter because acquired companies are often backlog factories: duplicated tools, inconsistent policies, manual workarounds, and a queueing problem disguised as "culture." Autonomous execution attacks the queueing problem—if governance exists.

## The Next Decade's Commercial Winners Will Look Calm, Not Busy

Most organizations will respond to this shift with more activity. They will run louder pipelines, heavier enablement, more dashboards, more internal coordination. They will call it rigor.

The agentic competitors will look quieter. Not because they care less. Because their operating model doesn't require constant human arbitration to stay coherent.

The "40–60% cost reduction" conversations are not surprising in environments where autonomous execution replaces manual queue work and exception handling becomes the human focus. What's surprising is that many leaders still treat these outcomes as automation wins. They are architecture wins. And architecture wins travel.

## The Enduring Advantage: Governed Autonomy as a Core Capability

By the end of this decade, autonomy won't be exceptional. It will be infrastructural. The question won't be: "Do we have agents?" It will be: "Can we run autonomy at scale without losing control?"

That is why the durable advantage belongs to companies that treat autonomous execution as core capability:

- They build approved lanes before they scale actions.
- They instrument outcomes before they believe narratives.
- They engineer rollback before they accelerate.
- They redesign roles before they flood the org with automation.

## The Challenge: Design the System Now, Before It Designs You

If you don't architect autonomous execution deliberately, it will still arrive. But it will arrive as sprawl:

- local automations,
- uncontrolled agents,
- conflicting definitions,

- brand drift,
- compliance panic,
- and leaders pulling the emergency brake after the first incident.

That is not transformation. That is a company being redesigned by its own contradictions—at machine speed.

The next decade will not reward the companies that "adopt AI." It will reward the companies that can govern autonomous execution as an operating system: one truth, one execution fabric, observable actions, controlled lanes, and humans positioned where judgment is irreplaceable.

Design it now. Because if you don't, you'll still get an autonomous organization. You just won't be the one running it.

# Chapter 25

# The Revenue Capital Reallocation Model

## The Shift Boards Will Actually Fund: Revenue Is Becoming a Capital Allocation Problem

For thirty years, revenue leadership treated growth as an employment plan. More SDRs. More AEs. More managers to inspect the machine.

That mental model is collapsing because the binding constraint is no longer activity. It is *system reliability under complexity.*

Agentic Revenue Systems force a brutal reframing: your revenue organization is not a sales team. It is a capital structure.

Once autonomy enters execution, you must decide where revenue capital belongs:

- in labor that produces activity, or
- in infrastructure that produces governed throughput.

Economic research on capital reallocation is blunt about what creates efficiency: resources move from low-productivity legacy structures into higher-throughput, higher-reliability systems as constraints bind and dispersion widens [https://www.aeaweb.org/content/file?id=17701]

[https://people.duke.edu/~rampini/papers/efficientreallocation.pdf]. Revenue is now experiencing the same logic. With fewer excuses.

## Spell It Out Brutally: If You Implement Agentic Revenue Systems...

### Do you hire fewer SDRs?

Yes. Not because SDRs are "bad." Because SDR headcount is old capital: expensive, constrained, and subject to diminishing returns when execution becomes instrumented and continuous.

Capital reallocation research shows that when resources can be reallocated efficiently, a large portion of losses comes from keeping too much capital in low-productivity uses—reallocation can eliminate the majority of those losses by shifting away from "old capital," aided by mechanisms that reduce the effective resale price and favor productive constrained units [https://www.aeaweb.org/content/file?id=17701].

In revenue terms: the SDR model was designed to manufacture coverage when the system could not run continuous outreach, qualification, follow-through, and routing on its own. Once the system can do those things inside guardrails, adding SDRs stops being capacity creation. It becomes coordination debt.

You will still need humans. But the SDR function shrinks and sharpens: less volume production, more exception handling, more high-context human moments, more signal validation.

### Do you reallocate budget from headcount to data infrastructure?

Yes. This is the real conversion.

Capital reallocation models explicitly prescribe subsidizing new investment and penalizing the persistence of old, low-productivity capital—because system-level efficiency depends on shifting the investment base, not polishing the legacy mix [https://www.aeaweb.org/content/file?id=17701] [https://people.duke.edu/~rampini/papers/efficientreallocation.pdf].

Revenue organizations will mirror this, whether they admit it or not:

- less spend on headcount growth as the primary lever,

- more spend on canonical data, identity resolution, event streams, governance tooling, observability, and policy enforcement.

This is not "IT modernization." It is installing the production plant for revenue execution.

**Does RevOps double in strategic importance?**

Yes. RevOps becomes the governance hub for signal integrity, allocation decisions, and the control surfaces that let autonomy run without incident.

Research on pecuniary externalities underscores why reallocation cannot be managed locally: when allocation decisions create external effects through prices, values, and constraints, governance becomes a central coordinating function rather than a peripheral reporting layer [https://wifpr.wharton.upenn.edu/wp-content/uploads/2023/09/Cui-Wright-and-Zhu.pdf].

In revenue: when autonomous systems can route, prioritize, suppress, and intervene, the "price" of bad definitions and bad signals is no longer internal argument. It is customer impact and forecast distortion. RevOps becomes control engineering, not dashboard production.

### Does enablement become AI governance?

Yes. Enablement stops being "content + coaching." It becomes the operating discipline that bounds autonomy, trains supervision behavior, and manages the exception-to-intervention ratio.

This is the underappreciated constraint logic: as autonomy rises, you must decide when humans intervene and when they do not. That boundary behaves like a collateral constraint in macro models: loosen it without controls and you get instability; tighten it without instrumentation and you get stagnation [https://www.nber.org/system/files/working_papers/w25085/w25085.pdf].

Enablement becomes governance because the organization's performance will increasingly depend on:

- how exceptions are defined,
- how interventions are executed,
- how overrides are audited,
- and how quickly the system learns without reverting to human theater.

## The Table That Reframes the Executive Conversation

| Legacy Model | Agentic Model |
|---|---|
| **Hire for activity** (scaling SDR headcount despite constraints and diminishing marginal returns) [https://www.aeaweb.org/content/file?id=17701] | **Invest in system reliability** (subsidize new data/infra; penalize persistence of old capital) [https://www.aeaweb.org/content/file?id=17701] [https://people.duke.edu/~rampini/papers/efficientreallocation.pdf] |
| **Manage pipeline via inspection** (manual oversight, high override frequency) | **Govern pipeline via signal architecture** (confidence scores, signal integrity, exception ratios) [https://www.irs.gov/pub/irs-soi/25rpcapprivfirmdyn.pdf] |
| **Add headcount to grow** (dispersion in marginal productivity; scaling creates coordination drag) [https://events.bse.eu/live/files/5421-p-martellinipdf] | **Increase throughput per seller** (reallocate to high-productivity; pairwise trades; raise baseline coverage) [https://events.bse.eu/live/files/5421-p-martellinipdf] [https://www.irs.gov/pub/irs-soi/25rpcapprivfirmdyn.pdf] |
| **Forecast via narrative** (variance driven by frictions and indivisibilities; late discovery) | **Forecast via system confidence intervals** (variance as a managed system output; reliability reported |

| [https://www.nber.org/system/files/working_papers/w25085/w25085.pdf] | continuously) [https://www.nber.org/system/files/working_papers/w25085/w25085.pdf] |
|---|---|

This is not "use AI." This is "rewire how revenue capital works." Boards recognize that sentence immediately because it changes the investment logic.

## The Revenue Reliability Index (RRI): The Scoreboard That Makes Autonomy Fundable

CFOs don't buy growth narratives. They buy predictability. Because predictability drives capital allocation, hiring, margin protection, and risk tolerance.

Agentic Revenue Systems win when they convert autonomy into *measurable reliability*. So we need a reliability construct that does not depend on optimism.

### Definition

**Revenue Reliability Index (RRI)** is a composite measure of whether the revenue machine is stable enough to run at higher autonomy without increasing volatility.

**Formula**

**RRI = (1 - Forecast Variance) × Pipeline Signal Integrity × (Exception-to-Intervention Ratio) × (1 - Manual Override Frequency) × Data Confidence Score**

**Component meanings (operational, not philosophical)**

- **Forecast Variance**: how wide the miss band is, by regime. The point isn't "accuracy after the fact." It's volatility containment under frictions [https://www.nber.org/system/files/working_papers/w25085/w25085.pdf].
- **Pipeline Signal Integrity**: whether stage, intent, stakeholder state, and risk signals reflect reality consistently enough to trigger actions without human translation. Dispersion data at the firm level is a reminder that variance and misallocation are structural, not anecdotal [https://www.irs.gov/pub/irs-soi/25rpcapprivfirmdyn.pdf].
- **Exception-to-Intervention Ratio**: the percentage of interventions that are triggered as exceptions (high-value decision points) rather than distributed as constant human babysitting. This

is the difference between governance and bureaucracy.

- **Manual Override Frequency**: how often humans have to correct system actions or system outputs. High override frequency is not "engagement." It's a control failure.
- **Data Confidence Score**: a quantified belief that identity, event freshness, lineage, and policy constraints are intact tightly enough for execution. Treat it as the credit rating of your revenue data.

### Why RRI becomes a board metric

As reallocation research makes clear, inefficiencies amplify through externalities; predictability matters because the cost of misallocation compounds beyond the local function [https://www.aeaweb.org/content/file?id=17701] [https://people.duke.edu/~rampini/papers/efficientreallocation.pdf].

RRI translates autonomy into a CFO-legible claim:

- We can increase speed without widening variance.

- We can reduce headcount dependence without increasing risk.
- We can let the system act because intervention is governed by exceptions, not panic.

## Transformation Path Under Constraint: The Stair-Step Most Companies Will Actually Survive

Most organizations cannot jump to governed autonomy. Not because the ambition is wrong. Because their current revenue capital is locked in old structures: headcount, manual process, semantic conflict, and inspection cadence.

Capital reallocation is constrained-efficient, not instantaneous. The transition happens in steps because constraints bind and frictions impose sequencing [https://www.aeaweb.org/content/file?id=17701] [https://people.duke.edu/~rampini/papers/efficientreallocation.pdf]. Revenue will follow the same staircase.

| Stage | Description | Budget | Org Redesign | KPI Evolution | Risk Exposure |
|---|---|---|---|---|---|
| **1: Assistive AI** | Partial augmentation. Humans still run the | 20% infra shift | RevOps triage | Activity-to- | Low (inspe |

| | workflow. The system accelerates tasks. | | | signal ratio | ction heavy) |
|---|---|---|---|---|---|
| **2: Structured Automation** | Workflow automation and "bilateral trades" in allocation logic: work routing becomes mechanized. | 40% headcount cut | Fewer SDRs, data teams up | Throughput/seller | Medium (frictions) |
| **3: Supervised Agents** | Agents execute defined plays with supervision. Exceptions become a first-class operating object. | Subsidy new cap | Enablement → governance | RRI baseline | Medium-high (overrides) |
| **4: Bounded Autonomy** | Autonomy expands in approved lanes, liquidity-like boosts in execution as constraints loosen under governance. | Tax old cap resale | RevOps strategic core | Forecast intervals | High (but contained) |

| **5: Governance by Exception** | Constrained-efficient system: autonomy is default; humans supervise exceptions; reliability becomes a designed property. | Full reallocation | AI-signal architecture | RRI > 0.9 | Minimal (externality fixed) |
|---|---|---|---|---|---|

The point of the staircase is not maturity theater. It is risk containment. Each stage expands authority only as control surfaces become real.

## One Brutal Failure Story: When Autonomy Outran Governance

This failure is common because it starts as an executive compliment: "We're moving fast."

A revenue team deployed autonomous outbound and follow-up across segments with inconsistent definitions of ICP, qualification, and suppression states. The system was productive. It was also incoherent. In week two, accounts began receiving conflicting messages—

multiple sequences, overlapping claims, mismatched timing.

The field noticed first. Then customer success noticed. Then legal noticed.

The rep reaction was not philosophical. It was operational:

- reps started overriding system actions manually, because they didn't trust what would be sent next,
- managers demanded approvals "for safety," reintroducing latency,
- RevOps was pulled into daily arbitration, not system design,
- the CFO froze expansion budget because predictability collapsed.

Not because the agents "weren't good." Because the operating model had no enforceable boundaries.

### What fixed it (and what leaders should learn)

- **They stopped scaling autonomy and started scaling constraints.** Approved lanes were defined by segment, action class, and irreversibility thresholds.

- **They made suppression a first-class control surface.** The system learned when not to act. This reduced buyer fatigue and internal collisions.
- **They instrumented overrides as a failure signal.** Manual override frequency was elevated to a governance KPI. Overrides were treated as system debt, not rep preference.
- **They converted enablement into supervision training.** Reps were trained on when to intervene, how to escalate, and what evidence changed system probability.
- **They reported RRI monthly to the CFO.** The conversation shifted from "AI risk" to "control maturity."

The team didn't need less autonomy. They needed autonomy that could be contained. That is the whole thesis, expressed as consequences.

## The Executive Implication: Revenue Capital Will Be Repriced Around Reliability

When capital reallocates, the organization eventually looks obvious in hindsight:

- fewer SDRs producing noise,
- more investment in data integrity and event-driven execution,
- RevOps elevated to governance and control engineering,
- enablement repositioned as autonomy supervision and policy discipline,
- forecasting rebuilt as confidence intervals with continuous verification.

This mirrors the central finding in reallocation research: efficiency emerges when capital moves from legacy, low-productivity uses into structures that increase throughput and reduce variance under constraint [https://www.aeaweb.org/content/file?id=17701] [https://people.duke.edu/~rampini/papers/efficientreallocation.pdf].

Agentic Revenue Systems don't just change how work gets done. They change what the company invests in. And when capital logic changes, operating logic follows.

Epilogue

# The Quiet End of the Revenue Org As You Knew It

## Autonomy Isn't the Story. Authority Is.

Most books about technological shifts end by predicting winners and losers. This one ends with a simpler claim: the definition of a revenue organization has changed.

Revenue is no longer an employment plan with a quota attached. It is an execution system with capital allocation consequences.

In the legacy model, growth was explained as hiring velocity. You bought output by adding humans, then you managed the volatility that followed. In the agentic model, growth is explained as system reliability: canonical truth, event-driven execution, governed autonomy, and humans positioned where judgment is irreplaceable.

This is why autonomy is inevitable. Not because the tools are impressive. Because the old operating model cannot carry modern complexity at competitive speed.

## The Board-Level Reframe: Revenue As Capital Structure

Boards have always cared about the same three things: throughput, predictability, and control. What changed is what produces them.

Economic research on capital reallocation describes the structural logic with uncomfortable precision: efficiency emerges when resources move out of low-productivity legacy structures and into higher-throughput systems—especially when constraints bind and dispersion widens [https://www.aeaweb.org/content/file?id=17701] [https://people.duke.edu/~rampini/papers/efficientreallocation.pdf].

Revenue has entered that moment.

In the legacy model, "old capital" was constrained headcount: SDR volume, manual inspection cycles, human coordination as the control layer. In the agentic model, "new capital" is execution infrastructure: data integrity, signal architecture, orchestration engines, governance mechanisms, rollback discipline.

This is not a preference. It is the direction of economic gravity.

## The Real Outcome of This Transition: Fewer Stories, More Proof

Most commercial organizations run on narrative because the system cannot verify itself. When forecasting is episodic and execution is human-timed, legitimacy comes from persuasion. That is why pipeline calls feel like court.

Agentic revenue systems replace persuasion with verification. And verification changes culture faster than any executive memo ever will.

This is also why forecasting becomes confidence intervals and control—not story and charisma. Research on frictions and indivisibilities makes the mechanism explicit: variance is structural when systems cannot reallocate and adjust continuously [https://www.nber.org/system/files/working_papers/w25085/w25085.pdf]. Your forecast stops being a declaration. It becomes a governed belief state.

## What You Actually Reallocate

If you implement agentic revenue systems seriously, you will make reallocations that feel politically offensive in the old model and mathematically obvious in the new one:

- **You hire fewer SDRs.** Not as a cost-cutting ritual. As a shift away from low-productivity "old capital" toward scalable throughput, consistent with reallocation logic that reduces losses by moving resources to higher-productivity uses [https://www.aeaweb.org/content/file?id=17701.
- **You move budget from headcount into data and control infrastructure.** Reallocation models explicitly point to subsidizing new investment and taxing persistence of old capital to improve system-level productivity [https://www.aeaweb.org/content/file?id=17701] [https://people.duke.edu/~rampini/papers/efficientreallocation.pdf].
- **You elevate RevOps into a governing function.** Because allocation decisions create external effects across the system; they cannot be

managed as local optimizations [https://wifpr.wharton.upenn.edu/wp-content/uploads/2023/09/Cui-Wright-and-Zhu.pdf].

- **You turn enablement into autonomy supervision.** Because constraint management—not motivation—becomes the performance bottleneck when execution is continuous [https://www.nber.org/system/files/working_papers/w25085/w25085.pdf].

None of this requires an ideology about AI. It requires a willingness to fund what now produces reliability.

## The Metric That Will Outlive the Tooling: Revenue Reliability Index (RRI)

Tool categories will churn. Vendor names will rotate. The scoreboard will not.

If you want autonomy to be fundable instead of fashionable, you need an index that translates autonomous execution into CFO-legible stability.

**RRI = (1 - Forecast Variance) × Pipeline Signal Integrity × (Exception-to-Intervention Ratio) × (1 -**

**Manual Override Frequency) × Data Confidence Score**

This is not a vanity construct. It is an economic translation:

- **Variance** is what frictions produce when systems can't adjust continuously [https://www.nber.org/system/files/working_papers/w25085/w25085.pdf].
- **Signal integrity** is what makes reallocation of attention and action reliable across dispersed performance regimes, consistent with empirical dispersion in firm outcomes [https://www.irs.gov/pub/irs-soi/25rpcapprivfirmdyn.pdf].
- **Exception governance** is how autonomy scales without scaling supervision cost.
- **Override frequency** is the clearest operational measure of whether the system is trustworthy or merely busy.

When RRI rises, the board stops asking whether autonomy is "risky." They start asking how fast you can responsibly widen approved lanes.

## The Endgame: Revenue Becomes a Governed Machine, Not a Managed Crowd

The most important conclusion of this book is not that agents will do more work. It's that management becomes a different discipline.

In the old model, leadership attention was the coordination layer. In the agentic model, leadership attention becomes the governance layer: decision rights, constraint design, exception economics, and continuous verification.

This is why the next decade of commercial winners will look unnervingly calm. Their teams won't be "more motivated." They'll be less dependent on coordination theater. They will run tighter loops with fewer surprises because the system closes gaps before the quarter turns into a rescue operation.

## The Final Choice

You do not get to choose whether autonomy enters revenue execution. You only choose whether it comes as:

- **sprawl**—uncoordinated agents, conflicting definitions, brand drift, governance panic, and slow retreat to human heroics,
- or **architecture**—one truth surface, approved lanes, observability, rollback, and humans positioned where judgment changes outcomes.

Capital will reallocate either way. The only question is whether it reallocates by design or by damage.

# About the author

Tim Cortinovis is a globally recognized agentic AI entrepreneur, keynote speaker, and thought leader. He was recently rewarded as a Top 10 Thought Leader Agentic AI and as a Top 10 Thought Leader Sales by Thinkers360.

Forbes called him a "tech visionary".

Fortune 500 companies' event attendees love his energetic way of telling stories that resonate. Since 2011, Tim has been traveling globally with keynotes and workshops in English, German, and Spanish to help companies use innovative technologies such as AI, the metaverse, or blockchain to grow exponentially.

Among his clients are companies like Siemens, Avaya, ING, Arvato or e.on.

He is a former TV news anchorman and has a university degree in linguistics.

His insights have been featured in Forbes, Fast Company, Inc. Arabia, International Business Times, and Les Echos. He has seven books to his name so far.

The quickest way to find him is on LinkedIn, where he posts (almost) daily insights into new technologies in sales and responds to his DMs:
https://www.linkedin.com/in/timcortinovis/

# Also from Tim Cortinovis:

**“The Single-Handed Unicorn: How to Solo Build a Billion Dollar Company”**

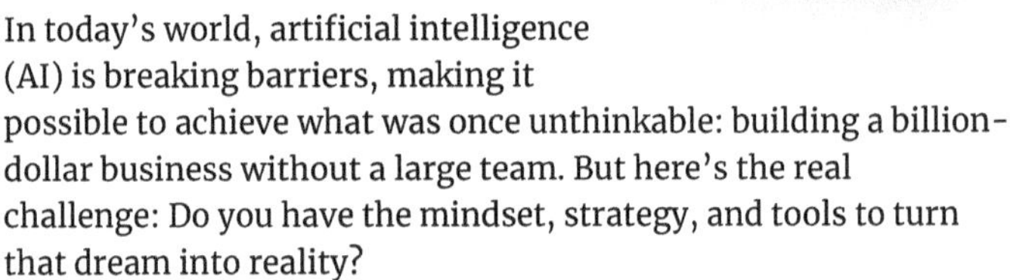


Read the whole story. Mindset, toolset, business models, strategies and tactics.

**#1 AMAZON BESTSELLER “tech visionary Tim Cortinovis" —Michael Ashley for Forbes**

**Build Your Dream, Scale Your Vision, and Become an AI-Powered Solo Unicorn**

In today’s world, artificial intelligence (AI) is breaking barriers, making it possible to achieve what was once unthinkable: building a billion-dollar business without a large team. But here’s the real challenge: Do you have the mindset, strategy, and tools to turn that dream into reality?

*The Single-Handed Unicorn: How to Solo Build a Billion-Dollar Company* is the definitive guide for ambitious solopreneurs who are ready to redefine business success. Whether you’re a freelancer, consultant, content creator, or startup visionary, this book is your step-by-step roadmap to leveraging AI, building resilience, and scaling your vision to extraordinary heights—all while flying solo.

Available as:

ebook
Paperback, 195 pages
audiobook
Buy the book on Amazon

Do you want this conversation inside your leadership team? Tim is available to speak in English, Spanish, and German.

Check Tim´s availability with Tim´s AI assistant Rick

rick@cortinovis.de

or

https://www.timcortinovis.com/book.

www.ingramcontent.com/pod-product-compliance
Lightning Source LLC
LaVergne TN
LVHW020517100826
845148LV00010B/1256